# 10
# Steps to
# Successful

## *Facilitation*

# Association for
# Talent Development

## 2nd Edition

PRESS

21  20  19  18           1  2  3  4  5

ATD Press is an internationally renowned source of insightful and practical information on talent development, training, and professional development.

ATD Press
1640 King Street
Alexandria, VA 22314 USA

Ordering information: Books published by ATD Press can be purchased by visiting ATD's website at www.td.org/books or by calling 800.628.2783 or 703.683.8100.

Library of Congress Control Number: 2018907842

ISBN-10: 1-949036-28-6
ISBN-13: 978-1-949036-28-2
e-ISBN: 978-1-949036-29-9

**ATD Press Editorial Staff**
Director: Kristine Luecker
Manager: Melissa Jones
Community of Practice Manager, Learning & Development: Amanda Smith
Developmental Editor: Jack Harlow
Text Design: Kathleen Dyson
Cover Design: Iris Sanchez and Shirley E.M. Raybuck
Printed by Data Reproductions Corporations, Auburn Hills, MI

# Contents

# Introduction

The art of facilitation is a necessary and evolving skill, and an important component of every professional's business acumen. Facilitation skills are essential today for all professionals dealing with any kind of work group, including management, boards of directors, top leadership, task forces, committees, and project teams. Facilitation involves processes and expertise that help groups to function effectively, including how they talk to each other, identify and solve problems, make decisions, and handle conflict. The facilitator guides the group to work together more efficiently—to create synergy, generate new ideas, and gain consensus and agreement—and guide them to a specific outcome. Facilitators point participants in the right direction, make suggestions, take steps to enhance the experience for the participants, and give guidance—but do not do the work for the group.

The fact is, facilitation is not about you—it is about the group. Standing in the spotlight as the facilitator can be a scary and daunting experience.

This second edition of *10 Steps to Successful Facilitation* provides an updated step-by-step guide for understanding your role as facilitator, planning your session, and walking through each milestone of a successful meeting, including techniques for accomplishing objectives and dealing with disruptive participants. We've reorganized the material to align with challenges facilitators face today, including the increasing prevalence of virtual meetings.

Use the key steps in this book as needed. For example, if you have been asked to facilitate a meeting with a predefined agenda, focus on steps 3–10. Or, if you have been asked to facilitate a group for a project in its infancy and you are faced with a completely blank slate, then it might be most appropriate to start with step 1 and work through all the steps systematically.

## Inside This Book

Each chapter of this second edition has been updated with new material. Our goal is to help you easily understand how to facilitate a productive meeting, prepare for and avoid any potential pitfalls, and hone an increasingly valuable business skill. In particular, this book delves into each of the following steps:

### Step 1: Understand the Role of a Facilitator

There are many myths regarding the role of a facilitator in helping a group achieve defined goals. For example, a facilitator is not a leader who directs what the group should do. This step delves into defining facilitation; the differences between facilitators, presenters, and trainers; the primary roles of a facilitator; and how a facilitator is chosen.

### Step 2: Plan the Facilitation Session

The goal of facilitation is to accomplish defined objectives. This step describes how to set up the meeting for success by identifying the client's goals, creating an audience profile, preparing an agenda, setting up meeting logistics—including selecting and arranging the room for optimal participation—and assigning any necessary pre-work to the group.

### Step 3: Begin the Meeting

With the groundwork laid, it's time to open the meeting, engage the participants, and help them to feel more comfortable with each other through icebreakers, if necessary (which can be especially important for virtual groups). A strong beginning also explains what the participants can expect throughout the session and helps reassure them that their valuable time will be respected with a purposeful, well-directed meeting.

### Step 4: Help the Group Generate Ideas and Make Decisions

Because a large percentage of a facilitator's time is spent helping groups generate ideas and make decisions, this step describes a wealth of updated tools and activities that successful facilitators can use to spark creativity, rank and prioritize solutions, and finalize decisions as a group.

### Step 5: Integrate Media and Technology for Impact

When facilitating a meeting, chances are that you'll need to leverage at least one type of media. This updated step describes the features and benefits of various types of media and visual aids to effectively facilitate sessions that clearly communicate information, capture ideas, and determine the best solutions.

### Step 6: Keep the Meeting Moving and Accomplish Objectives

This step involves facilitating the flow of the session, as well as using questioning techniques, tools, and activities to engage participants and ensure effective communication throughout the session. Most business professionals have experienced meetings that stagnate as participants push their own agendas; facilitators can keep it on track.

### Step 7: Leverage Strategies to Develop Teams and Deal With Conflict

Unfortunately, many facilitators encounter difficult participants who may be the "one bad apple to spoil the bunch"; or perhaps the entire group is a bit dysfunctional and apathetically goes through the motions without making any progress toward accomplishing the group goals. This step explores the stages of group development and the process of identifying and dealing with behaviors that can hinder group effectiveness.

### Step 8: Facilitate Virtually

Thanks to technology, participants no longer have to gather in person to hold effective meetings. This step, new for the second edition, describes the differences you can expect between facilitating a virtual rather than an in-person meeting, including how to ensure effective communication when you cannot see the participants (and they can't see you), and how to make sure you leverage the correct technology.

### Step 9: Close the Meeting and Follow Up

The end of the meeting is just as important as the beginning. Carefully planned closing activities, including a well-executed debrief session, will summarize the group's accomplishments, make its next steps clear, and allow the group to depart with a feeling of accomplishment rather than a muddled sense of lost time.

### Step 10: Evaluate the Facilitation Session

The last step in the facilitation process is to reflect on the session and evaluate how well you and the group achieved its goals. This critical step ultimately leads to continuous improvement and refinement of your facilitation skills. This step identifies several strategies for obtaining and analyzing information to evaluate the session's success.

Review these 10 steps as often as needed to build and perfect your ability to facilitate effective, performance-driven facilitation sessions.

*10 Steps to Successful Facilitation* is part of the 10 Steps series and was written to provide you with a proven process, quick reference tips, and practical worksheets to help you successfully facilitate any session or meeting. We hope that the tips and tools contained in this book will guide you each step of the way in developing and delivering an effective facilitation session.

# Step 1

# Understand the Role of a Facilitator

## Overview

- Define what facilitation is.
- Determine the differences among facilitators, trainers, and presenters.
- Clarify the roles and skills of a facilitator.
- Establish how facilitators are selected.

You've probably had some experience working in a group setting at one time or another. Groups, a basic work unit of organizations, are often tasked with providing a range of perspectives on an issue, solving problems, or coordinating complex work processes.

For many people, the experience is a mixed bag. At times, group members work well together—their thoughts, ideas, and approaches on how to get something done are similar, and the work flows. At other times the team flounders, struggling to identify basic goals and objectives, never coming to agreement, and eventually disbanding, feeling frustrated. What differentiates the successful groups from the inefficient ones? Facilitation.

# What Is Facilitation?

Facilitation is the art of moving a group of people through meetings, planning sessions, or training, and successfully achieving a specific goal. Typically, the facilitator has no decision-making authority within a group but guides the group to work more efficiently together, create synergy, generate new ideas, and gain consensus. How do facilitators accomplish all of this? By helping to improve a group's processes— how they talk to one another, identify and solve problems, make decisions, and handle conflict.

You don't have to be a professional facilitator to be asked to facilitate a group. Facilitators come from many backgrounds and may hold various roles within or external to an organization, such as leaders, managers, consultants, coaches, trainers, and formal facilitators. Anyone can appoint or hire a facilitator, for any type of meeting. You may be asked by a senior manager to mediate an internal meeting of your peers; as an executive, you may be asked to facilitate a series of meetings with a group in another department; you may be asked to facilitate a virtual meeting for a team that is scattered around the world and have never met; you may be asked as a volunteer to facilitate a community meeting or a meeting for a nonprofit that is important to you. And, of course, there's an entire industry of professional facilitators hired for meetings of all shapes and sizes.

Whatever the occasion, facilitation skills are essential for all professionals dealing with any kind of work group, including management, executive boards, senior leadership, task forces, committees, and project teams. The fact is, facilitation skills are assumed to be part of every professional's business acumen in today's work environment.

## POINTER

One of the key tenets of facilitation is that the process and experience is not about you—it is about the participants. The purpose of facilitation is to guide a group to an agreed-upon outcome. Facilitators point participants in the right direction, make suggestions, take steps to enhance the experience for the participants, and offer guidance—but do not do the work for group.

# What Are the Differences Among Facilitators, Trainers, and Presenters?

Facilitators assist teams in their meetings to improve how the team works together and comes to decisions, ensuring every voice is heard and conflicts are successfully resolved. In comparison, a presenter provides information to the group, typically in a one-sided delivery to an audience; for example, a presenter may report annual sales numbers or new HR policies to a group of employees. Trainers are also responsible for imparting information to their audience, but their goal is for the group to comprehend and retain the material, so training sessions are usually more interactive than a presentation. Trainers and presenters are also typically considered authorities on their subjects, but facilitators don't need to have any special knowledge about the subject of the meeting. Facilitators focus on the group dynamics and processes. Tool 1-1 overviews some differences in roles and responsibilities between trainers and presenters on the one hand and facilitators on the other.

Effective facilitators are accountable to the group; therefore, the facilitator must earn their trust. It's a different role from that of a presenter or trainer, where there is a clear and obvious separation between the students and the instructor, and in which the presenter is positioned as an expert. In that situation, the learners are merely passive recipients of the knowledge. In contrast, facilitators operate as impartial peers to participants; they must earn trust not through subject matter expertise, but their ability to successfully guide discussion and consensus while getting down into things alongside participants.

## POINTER

Facilitators are experts in the process of facilitation—not necessarily the content being discussed or decided on during the meeting.

## TOOL 1-1
### TRAINERS, PRESENTERS, AND FACILITATORS

| Trainers and Presenters | Facilitators |
|---|---|
| Deliver information | Assist with group discussions |
| Share their knowledge | Allow members of the group to share knowledge with one another |
| Are subject matter experts | Are not subject matters themselves, but support a group of participants who are |
| Focus on individual learning objectives | Focus on group objectives |
| Share the right information | Build consensus and agreement around decisions the group makes |
| Have a point of view | Are objective, nonjudgmental, not stakeholders |
| Direct, tell, inform, teach | Listen, question, coach |
| Control all facets of the session | Share control with the group |
| Derive credibility from demonstrating subject matter expertise and presentation skills | Derive credibility from using speaking, interpersonal, and questioning skills; managing the environment; sharing ideas; remaining flexible; and driving the group to agreement |

# Roles and Skills of a Facilitator

Facilitators wear many hats during a meeting—from managing the clock to making sure no one person dominates the meeting—all of which are critical to creating an effective experience. No matter which hats you wear, it is imperative that you remain objective when guiding the group. Skilled facilitators strive for excellence in three main areas: managing the facilitation process, acting as a resource, and remaining neutral.

Managing the facilitation process includes:
- following the agenda
- keeping members on task

- guiding the flow of contributions
- striving for consensus
- focusing on problem solving
- rewarding and motivating group members.

The facilitator acts as a resource to the group. This involves:

- advising on problem-solving techniques
- coaching for successful group behaviors and processes
- protecting group members from personal attacks.

It is essential that the facilitator remain neutral. This entails:

- staying emotionally uninvolved
- keeping out of the spotlight
- becoming invisible when the group is facilitating itself
- withholding personal opinions about the subject matter.

## Facilitator Skills

Facilitators can come from any background and a variety of experience levels. The best facilitators, however, demonstrate the following skills.

**Listening**—a facilitator needs to listen actively and hear what every team member is saying.

**Questioning**—a facilitator should be skilled in asking questions. Good questions are open ended and stimulate discussion.

**Problem solving**—a facilitator should be skilled at applying group problem-solving techniques, including:

- defining the problem
- determining the cause
- considering a range of solutions
- weighing advantages and disadvantages of solutions
- selecting the best solution
- implementing the solution
- evaluating the results.

**POINTER**

Good facilitators are:
- honest
- accurate
- clear
- informative
- interesting.

Notice that "entertaining" is not on the list. Remember, a facilitation session is not about you—it's about helping the participants achieve the desired outcomes.

**Resolving conflict**—a facilitator should recognize that conflict among group members is natural and, as long as it's expressed politely, should not suppress it. Indeed, it should be expected and dealt with constructively.

**Using a participative style**—a facilitator should be able to encourage all team members to actively engage and contribute in meetings. This includes creating an atmosphere in which group members are willing to share their feelings and opinions. This does not mean the facilitator should offer opinions on the content of the meeting, however.

**Accepting others**—a facilitator should maintain an open mind and not criticize the ideas and suggestions of group members.

**Empathizing**—a facilitator should be able to "walk a mile in another's shoes" to understand the team members' feelings.

**Leading**—a facilitator must be able to keep participants focused and the discussion on target.

## Extra Considerations for Virtual Facilitators

Meetings are not always held in person; increasingly companies are taking advantage of the many virtual meeting platforms to conduct meetings via videoconferencing tools. The role of a facilitator of a virtual meeting (a meeting that uses technology to gather a group of people who cannot meet in person because of distance or schedules) remains the same but is perhaps even more difficult. As a virtual facilitator, there are two additional considerations:

**Focus on clear, concise communication.** The lack of in-person communication makes building team rapport more difficult. Take care to make sure every participant has a chance to comment; consider keeping a list of participants nearby and making tally marks each time one speaks. If someone hasn't spoken in a while, ask for their comments by name. Also, do not let any one person dominate the discussion. During in-person meetings, participants can let someone know if they've been speaking too often or too long with body language, including shifting in their seats, rolling eyes, and beginning side conversations. In the absence of these gestures, it may fall to the facilitator to let a participant know when it's time to let someone else make a comment. Finally, ask questions to ensure the group has a common understanding of the issues; for example, "To summarize the last several minutes, we believe an increased social media presence should be the top priority. Is that correct?"

**Ensure the processes are working.** Try to incorporate at least two check-in points with the group to make sure the meeting flow and the technology is working for everyone. Ask once, about 30 minutes after the meeting has started, if anyone is having problems with the technology, hearing any speaker, or feeling lost. Check in again halfway through the meeting to make sure everyone is engaged and that the meeting processes are working for all participants.

## How Is a Facilitator Chosen?

Facilitators can be internal resources—from inside the company that's holding the meeting—or external, hired or appointed from outside the company. There are pros and cons to each type.

Sometimes, senior executives are appointed to facilitate a meeting. In addition to their experience, they may bring deep knowledge about the company, the issue at hand, and the decisions that would most benefit the company. Ironically, however, they can be among the worst facilitators because many people may be afraid to speak up in their presence. Participants may refrain from sharing their own thoughts, especially if they conflict with the senior leader's. Also, if a senior team member is expected to participate in the meeting, it's not a good idea for them to automatically be given the role of facilitator; it's too difficult to be both a fully functioning participant and a good facilitator.

> **POINTER**
>
> One of the most important roles of a facilitator is to draw out quiet participants and prevent other participants from dominating the discussion. To draw out quiet participants, consider:
> - asking by name if the person has anything to contribute
> - recognizing when someone has made a contribution
> - asking a question and having everyone respond to it at one time.
>
> To keep someone from dominating the discussion, interrupt gently and ask someone else for an opinion, or remind everyone of the time limits on agenda items.

If a senior leader isn't appropriate, the facilitator could be someone else within the company; choosing someone internal means the facilitator may understand the issues more quickly, saving time and money. In fact, companies often already have several individuals who have natural facilitation skills or have had facilitation training, although that might not be their primary job. This works if the internal facilitator is not part of the team who is meeting. Someone who is involved with the content of the meeting may have a hard time remaining neutral and may allow team members to go down a rabbit hole rather than sticking to the agenda.

If the outcome of the meeting is critical, time is of the essence, an unbiased leader is needed, and the team's full cooperation is necessary, a professional facilitator will bring the skills to get the job done. However, professional facilitators will require more time to learn about the company and the context for the meeting. Professional facilitators will also add an expense.

## What Types of Meetings Require Facilitation?

There are a variety of meeting types, several of which produce better outcomes when a facilitator, either internal or external, is used.

- **Standard weekly meetings**—Typically, these meetings do not require a facilitator. Highly functional teams, however, may appoint rotating facilitators, where the role shifts from one team member to the next each week.
- **Decision-making meetings**—These are also known as "critical outcome meetings," where the decisions or next steps affect the company in a major way. Use a facilitator, though preferably not someone who has a stake in the game, to keep the conversation productive and reach a decision with maximum buy-in from the group.
- **A meeting where neutrality is important**—As objective moderators, good facilitators can quickly earn the group's trust. Their objectivity also increases participation from the group and buy-in for the final decision.

- **Informational meetings**—If the goal of the meeting is to present information to a group of people quickly, rather than to gather input or gain buy-in, a facilitator is typically not necessary.

- **Creative meetings**—Sometimes a group of people need to get creative to solve a problem that has no obvious solution. A good facilitator will assist with brainstorming, managing the range of ideas created, and keep processes on track to eventually reach a conclusion.

Facilitators can be used for one-time meetings, or they may be called on to lead a series of meetings. Sometimes it takes more than one meeting to achieve the goal; a facilitator could meet with the same group of people several times or could meet with different groups of people all involved in the same issue. Although a wide range of circumstances benefit from a facilitator, all require the same skills.

Now that you have an appreciation of what a facilitator does and the responsibilities that accompany the role, use Tool 1-2 to evaluate your effectiveness and identify areas in which you can enhance your skills.

## TOOL 1-2
### FACILITATOR SELF-ASSESSMENT

Use this self-assessment to measure your readiness for the various roles of a facilitator and to identify areas for improvement. Using the scale provided, indicate to what extent you fulfill each of the roles listed below. For areas rated 1 or below, identify specific actions you plan to take to improve in that area.

0 = not at all

1 = to a very little extent

2 = to some extent

3 = to a great extent

4 = to a very great extent

| Role | Rating | | | | | Actions |
|---|---|---|---|---|---|---|
| | 0 | 1 | 2 | 3 | 4 | |
| Starts sessions on time. | | | | | | |
| Shares objectives with the group. | | | | | | |
| Maintains a positive, professional demeanor. | | | | | | |
| Remains neutral. | | | | | | |
| Manages the time to ensure all agenda topics are covered in the allotted time. | | | | | | |
| Creates and sustains an environment conducive for discussions and idea generation. | | | | | | |
| Helps participants to understand key concepts as they relate to the topics being discussed. | | | | | | |
| Listens actively. | | | | | | |
| Develops group cohesiveness. | | | | | | |
| Uses a variety of questioning techniques to generate discussion and facilitate deeper thinking. | | | | | | |
| Shares experiences that enhance credibility. | | | | | | |
| Helps others to identify problems. | | | | | | |
| Deals constructively with disruptive behaviors. | | | | | | |
| Protects group members from personal attacks. | | | | | | |
| Helps a group achieve consensus. | | | | | | |
| Promotes the development of action and follow-up plans. | | | | | | |
| Stops on time. | | | | | | |

# The Next Step

The next step in the process involves working with the client or primary contact to clarify the business objectives and the goals for the facilitation session, and to create an initial agenda.

# Step 2
# **Plan the Facilitation Session**

## Overview

- Understand the goals of the meeting.
- Create an audience profile.
- Prepare an agenda.
- Set up meeting logistics.
- Assign pre-work.

Now that you understand what facilitators are, it's time to explore how they prepare for what they do. Before the meeting even begins, facilitators are responsible for understanding its goals, assessing the needs of the group, planning and structuring the best activities, and setting up meeting logistics. We'll look at each of these tasks one at a time.

## Understand the Goals of the Meeting

When an opportunity to facilitate a meeting arises, spend some time up front to gather information that will help make the meeting successful. This includes having a conversation with your client (the person who asked you to facilitate). The purpose of this conversation is not to diagnose all the group's problems; rather, you should explore the client's motivation, previous experience with facilitators, and expectations for the meeting's outcome (Tool 2-1). This is also an excellent time to discuss ideas for facilitating this session.

## TOOL 2-1
### QUESTIONS FOR LEARNING CLIENT EXPECTATIONS

No matter what business need gave rise to the opportunity to facilitate a meeting, an initial conversation with your client or primary contact is essential. Here are some questions to ask:

- What are your goals for the outcome of this meeting?
- Use the SMART method as a framework to assess the goals. Are they:
  - Specific
  - Measurable
  - Achievable
  - Realistic
  - Timebound
- What do I need to know about this group? (For example, have they worked together before? Are they from different departments? Are they experienced or new to the company?)
- On a scale of one to five, how would you rate the communication within this group? One being not very good and five being excellent. (You can substitute "communication" for "collaboration" or "adjustments to change," or other considerations.)
- What are your concerns? What obstacles have you identified that might jeopardize a successful outcome?
- What, if any, progress has been made by the group so far? Has the group already agreed to any decisions?
- What next steps do you recommend?
- Have you worked with a facilitator before? If so, what can you tell me about the experience?

In that initial conversation, make sure you clearly understand the specific purpose for the meeting. Drafting the business goals and objectives not only clarifies your role but also helps to ensure that the client and you are on the same page. Together, create an outcome statement that is well defined and realistic according to the time constraints of the meeting. What does the client want as a result of the meeting: an agreed-upon decision? A recommendation? A prioritized list of ideas?

Although your client may want several specific deliverables by the end of the meeting, be careful not to pack in too much. Information or activity overload—giving too much news or asking people to solve too many problems at once—destroys meeting effectiveness (Tool 2-2). If necessary, consider holding two or more meetings to make sure you can accomplish all goals.

Whatever the purpose of the facilitation session, be sure to explain it to the group in advance, by email or any other communication method. Attendees should know ahead of time, for instance, whether they're expected to present recent sales data or to help solve a problem. Sharing the expectations for attendee participation helps to satisfy curiosity and allows participants to adequately prepare for the meeting.

## Tool 2-2
### Characteristics of Effective Meetings

No matter what the purpose, all productive meetings share similar characteristics. Use the following checklist to prepare for a successful facilitation session by ensuring the following:

- All participants have a valid reason for being included in the meeting.
- All participants know the purpose of the meeting and arrive prepared to fulfill that purpose.
- The meeting is as brief as possible, and there is an agenda to keep it on track.
- Participants understand their roles, respect the other participants, and feel responsible for the meeting content and outcomes.

- The meeting atmosphere is safe and supportive—participants feel free to express their views frankly, without fear of repercussion.
- Objectives—desired outcomes—are determined in advance, and there is adequate time to achieve them by the end of the meeting.
- All parties leave the meeting knowing what was accomplished and what is expected of them in the future, due to sufficient communication before, during, and after the meeting about goals and roles.

## Create an Audience Profile

Once you've established the *what* of the meeting—what it's about, and what it's meant to accomplish—you need to learn about *who* is involved. In an ideal situation, you should have all the information you need about your audience before you begin facilitating a meeting, so you can plan which facilitation techniques and activities will engage participants and help them reach their goals. It might be helpful to collect some information about the group's experience with the subject matter, working together, and their personal expectations for the session. You may gather this information from the client or ask the group members themselves in advance of the meeting (Tool 2-3).

### TOOL 2-3
#### AUDIENCE PROFILE

Try to gather the following information in advance, either from the client or directly from group members in the form of emailed questions:

- What is your experience with this project (skills, background, prior experience)?
- How do you feel about the topics we will be discussing?
- Do you work primarily by yourself or within a group?
- What are your expectations regarding this project?
- What are your expectations for our meeting?
- Do you have any suggestions for our meeting or ideas for discussion?

- In a typical workday, how many hours are you seated? (Use this question to shape the format of the meeting— participants who are used to being active most of the day may lose focus if asked to sit through a long meeting without interruptions or physical activities, for example.)
- Our meeting is currently scheduled for X:00. Where does this fall in your work cycle? (For example, are some of the participants just ending the graveyard shift and showing up for the session exhausted?)
- On a scale of one to five, how comfortable are you with change? One being very uncomfortable and five being very comfortable.

Whatever you ask of your participants, make sure that you give them enough time to answer your questions. If you do not have time prior to the facilitation session to identify this information about the participants, plan a warm-up activity to gather this information at the start of the session.

In the past, trainers and facilitators were encouraged to offer participants an assessment that would identify each individual's learning style, so they could prepare activities suited for everyone's needs. Today, it's enough to assume that you will have a variety of learning preferences in your meeting and plan a variety of activities to keep everyone involved, without needing to tailor them so specifically. The activities don't have to be complicated. For example, some participants absorb information easiest if they are provided with visuals such as an agenda, a list of issues, or a matrix for making decisions. Others learn best by listening to discussions and debating key points. Another group may need to be moving or doing something with their hands to get the creative juices flowing—accommodating them could be as simple as providing items to fidget with.

**POINTER**

For virtual meetings, especially if a group has not met in person, collect photos of everyone attending and create an introduction slide to help people put faces with names.

The most well-known learning preferences were first recognized by psychologist Howard Gardner in his 1983 book *Frames of Mind: The Theory of Multiple Intelligences.* He believed most people prefer to learn in one of the following ways:

**Verbal-linguistic learners** prefer using words, either written or in speech, and typically find it easy to express themselves. A verbal learner may enjoy any facilitation technique that involves speaking and writing, including role plays, especially with scripts, mnemonic devices, and acronyms, and debating pros and cons (either aloud or by writing down in lists).

**Logical-mathematical learners** prefer rational, analytical, scientific, and mathematical thinking. They can have strong reasoning, analyzing, and problem-solving skills. They also prefer information to be given in a methodical or linear order. A logical-mathematical learner may enjoy structured and goal-oriented activities that involve reasoning and logical sequencing, classifying and categorizing information, ranking brainstormed ideas, and statistics, graphs, charts, timelines, lists, and data reports.

**Auditory-musical learners** absorb information by listening and speaking. They prefer to hear content, including rhythmic words, alliterations, patterns, and music. To aid learners with an auditory

## POINTER

Keep in mind that people with different styles and preferences engage differently—facilitators must plan activities to work with their different needs and preferences. Here are three guidelines to help in addressing learning preferences and styles:

- Use techniques that appeal to at least two of the seven learning preferences in every activity. For example, if you provide instructions for an activity verbally and put them on a flipchart or a handout, you have hit the auditory and visual preferences at the same time.
- Change up often. By transitioning to a new topic or activity (or both) often and by changing the type of activity, you'll hit different combinations of preferences and styles throughout the meeting.
- Watch out for your own style. The activities you are most comfortable facilitating are most likely the ones that match your own learning style. If you're not careful, you'll tend to use those activities too much.

preference, consider incorporating spoken and auditory media, brain-storming aloud, or incorporating jingles and rhymes, background instrumental music, and question-and-answer sessions.

**Bodily-kinesthetic learners** absorb information through physical experiences. They have trouble sitting still for long periods of time and prefer to learn through direct involvement and hands-on activities. To aid participants with a kinesthetic learning preference, consider incorporating hands-on work, including creating lists, brainstorming, working with flipcharts and other media, role plays, and frequent breaks to stretch or take several laps around hallways to break up long periods of sitting.

**Visual-spatial learners** absorb information by seeing, viewing, and watching. They learn best from printed information, pictures, and graphics. Incorporate flipcharts, diagrams, charts, and videos into the facilitation session to accommodate these preferences.

**Interpersonal learners** are "people smart," and learn well in the company of others. Interpersonal participants will interact well and understand the perspectives of their fellow participants. They may volunteer to help you before, during, or after the facilitation session, and will be more engaged if you accept their offer. Interpersonal learners will thrive in environments with group projects and discussions and being asked to coach other participants.

**Intrapersonal learners** learn best when they are alone and can reflect on the information. They tend to be solitary and can analyze their own thoughts and feelings well. To help intrapersonal learners, consider incorporating time for independent thinking and give clear communication about why each activity or session goal is important for each participant.

Become familiar with a variety of facilitative methods and tailor them to the goals of your session. Though it can be a challenge to incorporate as many of these options as possible into the session simultaneously, doing so will help keep the session functioning well. Use Tool 2-4 as a guide for providing a range of activities to reach all of the learning preferences and styles in your meeting.

# TOOL 2-4

## ALIGNING ACTIVITIES WITH LEARNING PREFERENCES

| Facilitation Activity | Preference | | | | | | |
|---|---|---|---|---|---|---|---|
| | Visual Preference | Auditory | Kinesthetic | Verbal | Logical | Interpersonal | Intrapersonal |
| Presentation | x | x | | x | | x | |
| Handouts | x | | | x | | | x |
| Prioritize solutions | | | | | x | | |
| Group discussion | | x | | x | | x | |
| Role play | x | x | x | x | | x | |
| Group work at flipchart | x | x | x | x | | x | |
| Case study | | x | | x | | x | |
| Work with numbers or figures | | | | | x | | |
| Hands-on practice | | | x | | | | |
| Note-taking | x | | x | x | | | x |
| Games | x | x | x | | | x | |
| Small-group work | | x | | | | x | |
| Activity debriefing | | x | | x | x | x | |
| Action planning | | | x | | x | | |
| Brainstorming | | x | | x | | | |

# Prepare an Agenda

A meeting agenda lists the topics and the order in which they will be covered. Work with the client to determine the most logical sequencing of topics. As a best practice, send the agenda to participants along with the meeting invitation. This enables them to review the topics and prepare in advance. Consider these points when preparing your agenda:

STEP 2

- Cover the topics in order of importance, with the most important topic first. Doing so takes advantage of early-meeting energy and guarantees full coverage of the most important topics. The exceptions to this rule include when you need to logically sequence topics to lead participants down a path to understand all issues, or when it is helpful to give a quick status update or get administrative tasks out of the way.

- Schedule activities to cover each topic. For example, the activities for one topic may be group discussion and debate, whereas the activities for another may be brainstorming solutions for a problem.

- Try to end the agenda on a positive note—introduce something about which you expect to gain general approval from participants.

**POINTER**

When planning the facilitation session agenda, be as specific as possible. Each agenda item should be geared to accomplishing the business goal or objective of the meeting. If it is not, then consider whether it really belongs on the agenda.

After creating an agenda that lists the flow of all topics and activities, assign realistic timeframes for each activity for full participation by all attendees, and document it on the agenda (Tool 2-5). These estimates provide benchmarks to help keep the meeting on track and let you know if timing adjustments become necessary. The success of the session is usually based on whether the goals are all accomplished; time estimates will increase your odds.

# Tool 2-5

## Sample Agenda

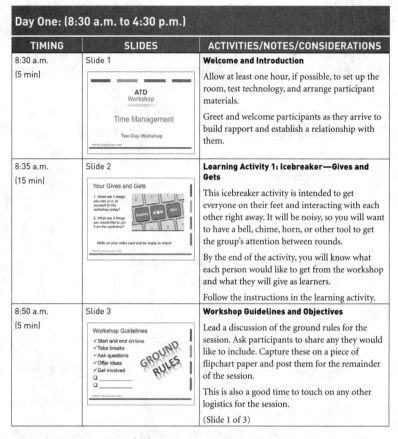

| Day One: (8:30 a.m. to 4:30 p.m.) | | |
|---|---|---|
| **TIMING** | **SLIDES** | **ACTIVITIES/NOTES/CONSIDERATIONS** |
| 8:30 a.m.<br>(5 min) | Slide 1 | **Welcome and Introduction**<br><br>Allow at least one hour, if possible, to set up the room, test technology, and arrange participant materials.<br><br>Greet and welcome participants as they arrive to build rapport and establish a relationship with them. |
| 8:35 a.m.<br>(15 min) | Slide 2 | **Learning Activity 1: Icebreaker—Gives and Gets**<br><br>This icebreaker activity is intended to get everyone on their feet and interacting with each other right away. It will be noisy, so you will want to have a bell, chime, horn, or other tool to get the group's attention between rounds.<br><br>By the end of the activity, you will know what each person would like to get from the workshop and what they will give as learners.<br><br>Follow the instructions in the learning activity. |
| 8:50 a.m.<br>(5 min) | Slide 3 | **Workshop Guidelines and Objectives**<br><br>Lead a discussion of the ground rules for the session. Ask participants to share any they would like to include. Capture these on a piece of flipchart paper and post them for the remainder of the session.<br><br>This is also a good time to touch on any other logistics for the session.<br><br>(Slide 1 of 3) |

*Used with permission from Downs (2016).*

## POINTER

Prepare meeting materials and handouts prior to the meeting. Ensure that they are free of errors (spelling or otherwise) and that you have enough copies for all participants.

# Set Up Meeting Logistics

It's a common scenario: The meeting room is too hot, the lights are too dim, the coffee is tepid, the projector does not focus, and the meeting participants are grumbling to one another.

The details of where a meeting is held and how the room is set up may seem minor—but these factors deeply affect the meeting's success. Rooms that are too small, uncomfortable, or not equipped properly can be stumbling blocks to an otherwise productive session.

Meetings can take place in a wide range of spaces, including theaters, storage rooms, classrooms, or restaurants. When selecting a room, be sure that the physical setting matches the meeting goals. Of course, in some cases, the client will arrange all logistics, including the room selection and food and beverages. If possible, discuss your preferences at your first meeting with the client.

Note that the rest of this step assumes you're facilitating an in-person meeting. For logistical advice on virtual meetings, see step 8. In the sections that follow, we'll explore some aspects of meeting logistics in detail.

## Seating Configurations

The placement of tables and chairs can influence the level of participation. Some seating arrangements make it difficult to interrupt the facilitator. Other arrangements encourage small-group activities. There is no single way to set up a room for a facilitation session, but some setups work better for certain kinds of meetings than others. Consider the following room setups when planning your session (Tool 2-6).

## POINTER

When you are asked what you want and need, never say, "Don't worry about me, any place is fine." Take advantage of the opportunity to have control over the room logistics and the ability to create a comfortable atmosphere to meet the session needs.

# TOOL 2-6
## ROOM SETUP MATRIX

| Style | When to Use | When Not to Use | Alternatives |
|---|---|---|---|
| Rounds | Larger groups<br><br>Work in teams<br><br>Small-group interaction<br><br>When using audiovisuals | Room too small<br><br>Group less than 15 | Classroom<br><br>Chevron |
| U-Shape | Smaller group size<br><br>Open environment<br><br>When using audiovisuals | Small room<br><br>Large group<br><br>Work in teams | Classroom<br><br>Chevron<br><br>Conference |
| Chevron | Large groups<br><br>For presenters who like to move<br><br>When using visuals | When a warm, personal atmosphere is needed | U-Shape<br><br>Rounds<br><br>Classroom |
| Conference | Small group<br><br>Group discussion<br><br>Formal and intimate | Room to spread out is needed<br><br>When using audio-visuals that require room<br><br>Presenter movement | Classroom<br><br>U-Shape |

## Rounds

Some people also refer to this configuration as "pods." In this setup, the facilitator and any audiovisual equipment are usually at the front of the room. Although the number of people at each table will vary, table seating averages between four and 10 people, depending on the size of the group. Rounds work well for groups of at least 15 people, especially when you want them to work in small teams. Setting up rounds requires a room large enough to allow ample space between the tables without chairs brushing up next to each other. The biggest challenge when using this configuration is that some participants may have their backs to the front of the room, requiring them to turn their chairs to see the facilitator or audiovisuals.

## U-Shape

This is popular for workshops. All participants can see each other, and the facilitator has plenty of room to walk around. This setup is particularly useful when you want to have small groups work together and works best for groups of 12 to 24 people, if the room is large enough. Be careful not to cram so many tables and chairs into a room that participants do not have enough space to leave the room when necessary.

## Chevron

This arrangement combines the best features of the classroom and rounds arrangements. Rows of tables are placed on angles and positioned behind each other, forming the letter "V" with a main aisle in the middle. Like the rounds setup, it makes for easy creation of groups.

This setup offers two main benefits. It can accommodate large groups, and because the tables are angled, participants can easily maneuver and walk around the room. This configuration also enables the facilitator to walk down the main aisle and use a variety of visual aids visible to the whole group.

If the group is large, the participants in the back of the room might have difficulty seeing some of the visuals. This setup also does not create an intimate environment, as most of the participants are looking at the backs of the people in front of them.

### Conference

This configuration involves the group sitting in chairs around a large conference table. The facilitator can take a seat at the table, either at the head for a stronger presence or at any chair for a more informal effect. This type of arrangement works well for both formal and informal meetings in which the group is relatively small, depending on the size of the room.

Keep in mind that some participants might be a bit confined if they cannot walk around the table. This setup is also not as conducive to group activities as rounds.

## POINTER

Assemble a facilitator's toolkit with the basics you'll need to facilitate the session in case the meeting room is not set up as you anticipated. Carry your own markers, sticky notes, index cards, and so on—whatever you will need for the session.

### Visuals

Now that you have everyone seated, you have to give them something to look at. Chances are you'll be using at least one type of media to support the meeting. Although visuals can clarify the issues and ideas, they can also turn the meeting into a disaster if you haven't appropriately planned for what you need. Prior to the facilitation session, make sure you have accounted for the following items:

- Verify that there are enough outlets to accommodate all audiovisual equipment needs.
- Arrange to have any extension cords or power strips you will need.
- Tape down or cover any cords or wires that might pose tripping or electrical hazards.
- Familiarize yourself with each piece of equipment before the meeting and cue up any visuals.
- Prepare a contingency plan if any equipment malfunctions, such as locating replacement bulbs or batteries.
- Know how to reach the on-site audiovisual contact should you need help.

Once you have your tech up and running, it's also important to make sure meeting participants can comfortably see any visuals you share. For the best size and placement of screens for display of visual aids, follow these guidelines:

- The distance from the screen to the last row of seats should not exceed six screen-widths.
- The distance to the front row of seats should be at least twice the width of the screen. Participants who are closer than that will experience discomfort and fatigue.
- The proper width of the viewing area is three screen-widths. No one should be more than one screen-width to the left or right of the screen.
- Ceiling height is important. The room's ceiling should be high enough—a minimum of nine feet—to permit people seated in the last row to see the bottom of the screen over, not around, the heads of those in front of them.
- If available, screens that recede into the ceiling and that automatically raise and lower are the best option.

## Plan for the Group's Comfort

Physical comfort in a meeting goes unnoticed if it's done correctly—participants can focus on the work. If the room is too hot, too cold, too dark, or the participants are starving, chances are they'll be too distracted to be effective. Here are a few specific comfort areas to focus on.

### Lighting

Lighting should create a comfortable environment for the audience. Not only does lighting affect the mood of the participants (primarily during the sleepy time after lunch), but it also determines how well the audience can see visual aids and their ability to take notes.

Make sure you know how to control the lighting.

- Find out what lighting operations are available at the meeting site either by asking the sponsor or by visiting the site prior to meeting day.

- Locate the lighting controls for all lights in the room and practice using the dimmer and slide switches.
- Determine what settings you plan to use during various segments of the meeting. For example, if you are going to go through introductions or an opening activity, make the lights bright. Dim the lights when appropriate to enable the group to see the visual aids easily.
- If you cannot access the lighting controls easily during the meeting, arrange to have someone sit by the controls to make the changes for you.

### Temperature

Prior to the meeting, be sure to find out how to control the room temperature. Can you adjust it yourself within the room or do you need to call someone within the building? Consider these guidelines:

- Begin with the room a little cool; the room will likely heat up as more people join the session and because some audiovisual equipment tends to throw off heat.
- For a daytime meeting in a room with windows, consider the effect of sunlight on the room temperature. Adjust the curtains or blinds—and perhaps the thermostat—accordingly.

## POINTER

The noise level outside your room can affect the meeting, especially if you're located in a hotel or conference center. If your room is separated from another room by a partition, or if it's near the kitchen entrance, check the noise level. If the noise is unacceptable, address the issue with the client or the facility contact.

### Food and Breaks

It's common for a light meal or snacks to be available in the meeting room or immediately outside the door. In fact, you might even be asked to conduct a facilitation session through lunchtime or at a dinner meeting. Because food service can affect the meeting, consider the following:

- Get to know the people who are handling the food service, and, if you are allowed any input, be clear about your expectations regarding when, how, and where the food will be set up.
- If possible, opt for lighter fare, such as fruit or pasta salads and small sandwiches. Heavier food tends to make people drowsy, especially right after lunch or in the late afternoon. Arrange for plenty of bottled water and juices as alternatives to sodas, as well as both decaffeinated and caffeinated coffee and tea.
- Ask for the food service to be set up in advance so that it does not interfere with the meeting. If this is not possible, arrange for the food to be set up outside the meeting room to minimize the noise and disturbance.
- Ascertain if any meeting participants have specific dietary restrictions or allergies and try to make accommodations for their needs or provide an opportunity for them to get their own food.

All of this planning—from room configuration through food service—should be done days or weeks ahead of the meeting. The day of the meeting, make sure you arrive in the meeting space before the participants and allow enough time to make sure the room is set up correctly. Also, display meeting objectives and the agenda, using a flipchart or other visual. If you'd like the participants to help define session objectives and goals, post blank flipcharts around the room.

## Assign Pre-Work

Most meetings involve some pre-work for the participants to complete. For virtual meetings, pre-work is almost always essential; virtual meetings tend to be shorter than in-person meetings, and therefore participants must come prepared.

Appropriate pre-meeting activities include reading documents or researching information to make the most effective use of the facilitation session time. This work is typically done several days or weeks before the meeting, at the convenience of the participants, which hopefully leaves time for deeper thinking. Follow these steps to prepare pre-work:

1. Ascertain whether people need to gather specific information that will be necessary to have in the meeting, such as research on a client, a competitor, or a new market. Are there any statistics or data that need to be prepared and brought to the meeting? Do participants need to complete a survey, of which the results will be shared during the meeting? Do they need to bring ideas about a particular topic?

2. If appropriate, make any sessions materials available before the meeting—documents, spreadsheets, reports, sales results, or a presentation deck—so participants can review the material and prepare feedback.

Make sure you give enough time for the participants to complete any pre-work. Also consider the audience and make sure the material is consistent with what they review in their normal course of work.

Not all meetings need pre-work. Assign pre-work only when it will benefit the team to have additional time to review and consider the material. Also, make sure to send out friendly reminders as the day of the meeting approaches, to help increase the number of participants that complete the pre-work.

## Get Yourself Ready

When preparing to facilitate a meeting, remember to consider your own needs, too! Start with a run-through. The time you spend practicing is usually proportional to the level of relaxation you experience the day of the facilitation session. Rehearse what you are going to say at the opening of the meeting. Memorizing the first few paragraphs will reduce your stress level and get the facilitation session started on the right foot.

Consider some of these techniques to help ensure you're prepared and to reduce jitters:

- **Practice in front of a mirror**—Some facilitators find this technique helpful, but it may subtly reinforce the notion that you're talking to and for yourself rather than the group.

- **Record yourself**—A video camera gives you an opportunity to observe your body language as well as hear yourself; however, like listening to a recording of your voice, a video may feel awkward to watch when reviewing your facilitation skills.

- **Perform to a friendly critic**—This technique puts the emphasis on projecting to a group. Be sure that the critic understands what you are trying to do and what their role is in providing you with feedback or reacting to the facilitation plan and flow.

- **Focus on nonverbal aspects**—Although most facilitators practice what they plan to say, don't forget to practice making eye contact (looking away from your notes and the facilitation plan at different points around the room) and using hand gestures, voice inflection, and your body language in general.

- **Do a dress rehearsal**—Find out if you can schedule time to practice in the room where the facilitation session will take place. Even if you cannot rehearse in the meeting location, be sure to practice with visuals, handouts, and any other materials that you need to synchronize with the facilitation session flow and discussion. This is especially important if you plan to use more than one type of media.

## The Next Step

Use the checklists in Tools 2-7 and 2-8 to make sure the meeting site will be conducive to a great meeting and that you and the participants will be fully prepared. Then, with your facilitation plan in hand, the next step is to begin the meeting.

# TOOL 2-7
## FACILITATION SITE GUIDELINES

To ensure the facilitation session location will promote interaction and support planned activities, follow these guidelines. Keep in mind that for longer meetings, comfortable chairs are essential.

### Location

- Is the meeting room located away from high-traffic areas, such as a kitchen or lobby, that might lead to interruptions?
- If necessary, are there signs directing participants to facilitation sessions, breakout rooms, or break areas?
- Is there a system set up to minimize outside interruptions?
- Have all telephones been disconnected from inside the meeting room, if necessary?
- Can you easily control the temperature and ventilation in the room?

### Room Size and Shape

- Do you have a space that is big enough to comfortably accommodate all participants?
- Do you need any special seating arrangements?
- Is there enough room for audiovisual equipment?
- Is there enough clearance between tables and chairs?
- Are doorways wide enough for audiovisual equipment and disabled participants to easily pass through?
- If any breakout rooms are to be used, do they all have the equipment and supplies required, and are they close to the main meeting room?
- If you will be leaving the meeting room for a lunch break, can you secure the room to ensure that materials, laptops, or other valuable items are safe?
- What arrangements do you need to make if the meeting takes place over breaks or multiple days to ensure that cleaning crews do not throw out flipcharts, handouts, or other materials that might be on the walls and tables?

### Room Functions, Features, and Technology

- Can the walls accommodate charts and panels?
- Are the ceilings high enough to accommodate projection screens?
- Do the walls contain enough electrical outlets (at least every eight feet)? If laptops are to be used, will anti-surge electrical outlets be needed?
- Will the facility have extra extension cords available or do you need to supply them?
- Are light switches easily accessible?
- Can different parts of the room—for example, at the front of the room near the screen—receive different kinds of lighting?
- Have you tested all the in-room audiovisual equipment?
- Have you tested the Wi-Fi or other Internet access, if necessary?

### Noise Control

- Is the room too close to the street?
- Is the room near an alleyway or loading dock?
- Is the room located near a building renovation or where heavy machinery is being used?
- Are elevators too close to the room?
- Is a noisy session scheduled for the adjoining room?
- Is there a dividing wall that does not shut out noise from the adjacent room?

### Furniture

- Do chairs have wheels that permit them to be moved without noise?
- Depending on the size of the group, are swivel chairs available?
- Do chairs have armrests that allow people to rest their arms at a 90-degree angle?
- Are there sufficient whiteboards or flipcharts, as well as markers?
- Can the tables be moved?

STEP **2**

# TOOL 2-8
## COUNTDOWN TO SUCCESSFUL FACILITATION CHECKLIST

Use this final countdown checklist to ensure that everything will go off without a hitch the day of the facilitation session.

**Two or More Weeks Before the Meeting (Start as Soon as Possible)**

❑ Meet with client to confirm the meeting objectives and create an audience profile.

❑ Make the room arrangements, including requesting equipment, supplies, and refreshments.

❑ Create the meeting agenda, the facilitation plan, and all visual aids.

❑ Send requests for any pre-work and any necessary materials to participants.

❑ Select the type of facilitation techniques you want to use to create interactivity.

❑ Develop the specific questions to ask the group and plan the activities to generate ideas, reach consensus, and achieve the meeting objectives.

❑ Make a list of all supporting materials that you need (for example, handouts or worksheets).

❑ Do a run-through and fine-tune the facilitation plan.

**One Week Before the Facilitation Session**

❑ Confirm that you have the right date and time of the meeting.

❑ Identify the on-site audiovisual contact for an in-person meeting; identify a technical support contact for virtual meetings.

❑ Confirm that participants have received the meeting invitation and any necessary technical information for a virtual session.

❑ Confirm that the room and set-up arrangements you indicated will be ready for meeting day.

❑ Rehearse the facilitation session flow with a friendly critic and ask for feedback and ideas.

❑ Make any final adjustments to the facilitation plan.

❏ Memorize the opening of the facilitation session and how you plan to transition to other topics or activities during the meeting.

❏ Practice using all audiovisuals. If using presentation software, click through all of the slides to remember where any special effects, such as dissolves, animation, or sounds, occur in relation to your notes. Check for any misspellings.

❏ If necessary, send presentation materials and any supplies ahead of time and check to be sure that they arrived.

**Meeting Day**

❏ Arrive at least 30-60 minutes prior to the facilitation session time.

❏ Make sure any materials that you sent ahead of time have been delivered to the meeting room.

❏ Test all equipment.

❏ Tape down cords or power strips to prevent tripping hazards.

❏ Arrange your facilitation plan, notes, handouts, and other session materials: tape, markers, and so on.

❏ Get a glass or bottle of water and paper towels.

❏ Scout out the restroom location.

❏ Arrange participants' handouts at their seats or on tables.

❏ Tidy up the room by hiding empty boxes and so on.

**Before You Begin the Facilitation Session**

❏ Review the first 90 seconds of your opening.

❏ Do deep breathing and stretch techniques to help you relax.

❏ Run through your visualization: Envision success and how you want the session to flow.

❏ Greet the participants.

STEP **2**

# Step 3

# Begin the Meeting

## Overview

- Develop a strong opening.
- Establish the ground rules, goals, and the parking lot.

With the groundwork laid, it's time to begin the meeting. Successful facilitation sessions open with a bang to get everyone on the same page and engaged in achieving the meeting's objectives. A strong opening includes using icebreakers, reviewing the agenda, clarifying the purpose and objectives, establishing ground rules, and explaining the parking lot.

## Develop a Strong Opening

The opening of a facilitation session should not only help to establish the credibility of the facilitator but also accomplish three things: Grab the participants' attention, express the main goal of the meeting, and explain what the audience can expect to get out of the facilitation session.

The first 90 seconds of a facilitation session sets the tone for the rest of the meeting. If you start off on the right foot, chances are you'll continue along that path. If, however, you start off on the wrong foot, it can be difficult to recover. It's all about being prepared.

In the first 90 seconds, be sure to:

- Look like you're confident, even if your knees are shaking. Acknowledge the group, smile (if appropriate), and start talking.
- Avoid reading from a script. Either memorize what you want to say or begin by asking questions of the participants.
- For virtual meetings, speak in a clear, confident voice. Also, consider asking each participant to remove any distractions from their field of vision.

Once you've used the first 90 seconds to set the right tone, it's time to warm everyone up.

How often have you attended a meeting that quickly fell flat after the housekeeping details were discussed? This might not have happened if the facilitator had used an icebreaker. Icebreakers immediately get people involved, foster interaction, and inspire creative thinking. There are two main types of icebreakers: openers and acquainters. The next two sections provide some ideas for each. You may need to personalize these ideas so they apply to the session. Of course, there are meetings in which icebreakers and acquainters would not be appropriate, especially formal meetings, such as a board of directors meeting, or recurring meetings, such as a weekly sales meeting where participants already know each other.

## Openers

Openers are intended to set the stage, ease into the session, and generally make participants comfortable. They're not just for the beginning of the session, either. An effective opening bridges what the participants were doing to the tasks at hand and may energize groups after coffee breaks or lunch.

Keep in mind, if your opener does not tie into the topic, you will only confuse and distract the participants. Some suggestions for openers include:

Ask questions to stimulate thinking on the meeting topic. These might be rhetorical questions or requests for a show of hands. Besides stimulating the thought process, this technique helps participants to focus on the topic.

Share a personal experience or anecdote. You will spark participant interest if participants have experienced something similar. But limit your "war stories"; too many can turn listeners off instead.

Give a unique demonstration. This works well with technical topics. You can then proceed from the introduction to explanations of the "why" and "how" of the demonstration.

Use an interesting quotation, or perhaps modify a well-known quotation to fit the topic. For example: "Ask not what work teams can do for you, but what you can do for your work team."

Relate the topic to previously covered content. Perhaps the speaker who preceded you, if another person gave an introduction, has established the groundwork for your meeting topic.

## Acquainters

Acquainters work well for small-group meetings where the participants do not already know each other. These icebreakers serve two functions: they establish nonthreatening introductory contacts, and they increase participants' familiarity with one another. Acquainters may have no relation to the topic of the meeting. They are designed to put participants at ease and relieve the initial anxiety that comes with any gathering of people new to one another. You can personalize the following acquainters for your group.

### Fancy Saying

This activity challenges participants to "translate" written communications. For example, project the following on a screen and have them decode the meaning.

- "A feathered vertebrate enclosed in the grasping organ has an estimated worth that is higher than a duo encapsulated in the branched shrub." (A bird in the hand is worth two in the bush.)
- "It is sufficiently more tolerable to bestow upon than to come into possession." (It is better to give than to receive.)
- "The medium of exchange is the origin or source of the amount of sorrow, distress, and calamity." (Money is the root of all evil.)
- "A monetary unit equal to 1/100 of a pound that is stored aside is a monetary unit equal to 1/100 of a pound that is brought in by way of returns." (A penny saved is a penny earned.)

### The Question Web

Post a list of 20 questions somewhere in the room and ask the participants to stand in a circle. Hold on to the end of a spool of string or a ball of yarn and throw the ball to someone. That person then has to select a question and answer it. Holding a segment of the string, they then throw the rest of the ball to another member of the group. Eventually this creates a web.

Here are a few example questions. Adapt these for your group or invent your own:

- If you could go anywhere in the world, where would you go?
- What did you want to be when you were a child?
- If you didn't have to sleep, what would you do with the extra time?
- If you could talk to any one person, living or dead, who would it be and why?
- Tea or coffee? Why?

### Name That Person

Divide the group into two teams. Give each person a blank card and ask them to write five little-known facts about themselves. For example, "I played hockey in college, I was born in Iceland, I love to bake, I have a pet bird named Tweety, and I have never ridden a bicycle." Collect the cards and divide into two piles by team. Taking turns, each team will draw one card from the opposing team's pile. Each team tries to identify the person in as few clues as possible. Five points if they guess correctly on the first clue, then four, three, two, one, and zero on subsequent tries. The team with the most points wins.

## People Bingo

This activity is great for groups who don't know each other well. Make a 5 x 5 grid on a card and write descriptive statements in each box. Make copies for everyone in your group. Encourage the group to mix, talking to everyone to try and complete their card. If one of the items listed on the bingo card relates to the person they are talking with, have them sign their name in that box. End the activity after 10 minutes and review some of the interesting facts the group has discovered about each other. Adapt the statements in Tool 3-1 for your group.

# TOOL 3-1
## PEOPLE BINGO

Circulate until you've found as many of the following people in the room as possible, asking them to sign the square that describes them.

| Has brown eyes | Speaks a foreign language | Has two or more siblings | Is over six feet tall | Played a sport in high school |
|---|---|---|---|---|
| Has made the longest journey | Plays a musical instrument | Name begins with an S | Has been on TV | Has gone bungee jumping |
| Likes to stay up late | Has the most pets | Loves to ski | Has only lived in one state | Has a set of twins in their family |
| Is wearing blue | Has been to the most foreign countries | Loves to cook | Was born in May | Likes to get up early |
| Loves to read | Wears glasses | Is left handed | Prefers tea over coffee | Plays tennis |

## Acquainters for Virtual Groups

If your team is meeting virtually, acquainters can be even more important because of the lack of opportunities for informal conversations and nonverbal communication, which often do the work of building trust and opening the lines of communication. Acquainters also give everyone the chance to speak at the beginning of the meeting, which increases the likelihood they will speak up again later on.

While some groups may already know each other, most of the time virtual work groups are convened because of distance, and the participants may never or rarely get the chance to meet in person. Consider the following acquainters to help your group establish rapport over computer screens and telephone lines. Adapt as necessary for your group.

### Show and Tell

Before the meeting, ask each participant to take a picture and email it to you. The picture can be the participants' choice, or can be a specific request. For example, you may ask everyone to send a picture of their shoes. Upload the pictures and share one at a time. Ask the owner of each pair of shoes to talk about their choice; for example, boots may indicate cold weather in one part of the country, sandals may indicate warm weather, and sneakers may indicate a running hobby. Or, you may ask the participants to take a picture of the weather outside their window, or of a favorite object on their desk. Use the photos as a basis for brief conversations.

### Virtual Tours

For small teams using videoconferencing platforms, ask for a quick (30-second) virtual tour of their office space. This can be done either by a participant walking their laptop several steps in each direction and pointing out features of their space, or by a participant simply explaining what is visible to them: what pictures are on the wall, what's outside the window, or a pet sitting at their feet in a home office. This is especially helpful to establish relationships for groups that will meet virtually frequently.

### Quick Questions

This works well when you have a large group or if time is short. Ask each person to answer a question in one sentence. You can pose the same question to the group or vary the questions.

Questions might include:

- If money and time were no object, where would you most like to go on vacation?
- What does the weather look like where you are? (If possible, ask for a photo to be sent and share with the group.)
- What was your first job?

### Two Truths and a Lie

Ask each team member to prepare a list of three interesting statements about themselves, one of which must be made up. Team members must guess which statement is the lie. For example, "I can play the guitar, I grew up on an island, and I have a sister who is 15 years older than I am." Whoever is able to fool the most people wins.

## Establish the Ground Rules, Goals, and the Parking Lot

From the very beginning of the session—or ideally, even before—participants should clearly understand the goal of the meeting, what the task is, why they are here, and how much time they have. These are accompanied by an explanation of ground rules and the parking lot.

The most successful facilitators usually provide a handout or display a flipchart detailing the agenda and estimated timing. This is an excellent point in the process to explain the planned approach to achieve the meeting outcomes. Spend a few minutes at the beginning to check for participants' understanding and agreement. Often participants may want to modify or add to the outlined topics or process. Try to gain group consensus, because it is really the group

> **POINTER**
>
> Begin and end all meetings on time. Late-coming participants will quickly learn that you do not hold the meeting for stragglers, and everyone will appreciate ending at the appointed time.

that will be performing the work and achieving the goals—as a facilitator you are a guide on their journey. Then, let everyone know how you'll get there together, by sharing the ground rules.

## Establish Ground Rules

Ground rules are behavioral expectations that facilitators and participants have of each other. It is best to write out ground rules and display them every time the group meets. Don't shortchange this process. The upfront time spent is well worth the investment. Not only do ground rules help to keep discussions on track, they also promote and maintain friendly group relations.

Developing ground rules can be an excellent opening activity. You can either:

- Present a list of proposed ground rules and facilitate an activity in which the participants react to and revise them.
- Facilitate an activity in which the participants propose their own ground rules and then come to a consensus or vote on them.

The best way to get buy-in is to have the group define its own ground rules for the meeting. If you choose this path, however, make sure you have already created a list of essential ground rules and keep it within your notes. Let the group list their own rules, but if you feel they have overlooked anything critical you can suggest a rule and ask them to consider how they would like to handle it.

To help you get started, consider using some of these ground rules for your facilitation sessions:

- Meetings begin and end on time.
- Attendees must actively participate.
- Only check phones and laptops at designated times.
- One person speaks at a time.
- No side conversations are permitted.

**POINTER**

Clarify the group's responsibility. As a facilitator, you enable the group to accomplish the stated goals and objectives. Make it clear to the group that your role is to help them identify issues, generate ideas, and decide on the best course of action. However, it is their responsibility to do the work. The group needs to clearly understand their responsibility and feel empowered to make decisions so they can actively engage in the process.

- Respect others and their opinions, even if different from yours.
- Speak up if you have something to say.
- What is said in this room is confidential and stays within the group.
- The group needs to come to a consensus when making decisions. If necessary, the group will vote to come to an agreement.

Once the group establishes and agrees to the ground rules, post them so that they are always visible. Quite often groups will "self-police," which means participants call each other on the ground rules when one is broken. Depending on the formality of the environment, the self-policing method can be as low key as simply pointing out infractions verbally, mentioning a key word, or throwing paper wads or Nerf balls at the offender.

## Establish the Goals of the Meeting

The goal of the meeting is not just to get through the meeting. You should already understand the goals of the meeting based on your initial interview with the client. Any information you were able to gather about the participants will help you understand their expectations and prior experience, and how those factors might help or hinder progress toward the goal. When discussing the purpose and objectives of the meeting, be very clear about what the group needs to accomplish by the end of the day, whether it's to finalize a decision, brainstorm ideas, or provide a list of possible solutions. Make sure to ask if there are any questions or concerns about the group's ability to achieve the day's goal.

> **POINTER**
>
> Identify the business goals and objectives of the facilitation session. If a clear purpose for the meeting or facilitation session is not provided, beware! Identify at least one or two outcomes, so that even if no other issues are addressed, the meeting is still deemed a success.

Reviewing the agenda is not the same as discussing the goals for the meeting. While a review is helpful at this point to get consensus for how the group will achieve those goals, a separate discussion to identify the deliverable itself is essential.

## Create a Parking Lot

The parking lot—a blank sheet on a flipchart, poster board, or other visible area—establishes a designated place to collect ideas or topics that are off the agenda as you go through the day. These are ideas the group values enough to visit at a later date. For example, if, during a discussion about a client, the team begins to debate the pros and cons of building another satellite warehouse to accommodate them, you might suggest that discussion seems worthwhile, but best suited for another meeting. You, or another note-taker, may list it on the parking lot, visible to all.

By documenting these items, the participants can acknowledge any ideas or questions that need to be addressed later and maintain focus on the current tasks. Placing items in the parking lot enables the group to keep moving forward while avoiding tangents that sidetrack the group's progress. At the end of the meeting, the group can determine if the parking lot items should be included in future meeting agendas or if any action is required by group participants outside of meetings.

This may seem like a lot to juggle in just the first few minutes of a meeting, but you can put all these steps into action by using the following checklist (Tool 3-2).

## TOOL 3-2
### BEGINNING A FACILITATION SESSION CHECKLIST

A productive facilitation session does not necessarily begin once every participant arrives; it begins at the time scheduled. Use this checklist to get you through the first few minutes of any facilitation session, at the time it is scheduled to begin. This checklist will help you manage those important minutes effectively.

- **Do not stop and restart the meeting**—The participants arriving on time recognize that you are ready for them and that you don't intend to waste their time. This recognition helps to set the tone for a productive meeting.

- **Display enthusiasm**–Be energetic and upbeat from the start and maintain your enthusiasm throughout the meeting.
- **Make sure everyone knows each other**–Introduce any participants who are new to the group. Use structured icebreakers to help everyone introduce themselves and learn more about the other participants.
- **Review the meeting objectives and agenda**–If this is the first time the group is meeting, then solicit a list of ground rules from the group and display them during subsequent meetings.
- **Appoint participants for key tasks**–Enlist help for activities such as keeping track of time and recording meeting notes.

## The Next Step

You've done your homework and already put it into action as you warm up the room, set ground rules, and begin the meeting. Now it's time to get into the meat of it—helping the group generate ideas and make decisions.

# Step 4

# Help the Group Generate Ideas and Make Decisions

## Overview

- Use different idea generation tools to get different results.
- Apply the appropriate method to make decisions.

Effective team decision making doesn't just happen—it's hard work! A large percentage of a facilitator's time is spent helping teams make decisions: from generating the ideas for solutions, to debating the pros and cons of each, to agreeing upon the best option. The assumption that groups can figure it out on their own is unrealistic and can set the team up for failure; and yet, teams are frequently unaware of, or unpracticed in the use of, idea-generating and problem-solving methods. Without a process to follow, there is ample opportunity for groups to get sidetracked, form competing alliances, or permit emotions to run amok. This step describes techniques to facilitate group problem solving and decision making.

Before a team can make a decision, they must first evaluate the options. Often, this begins with generating ideas. Most of the idea-generating and decision-making activities listed in Tool 4-1 work for virtual groups as well as in-person groups. For virtual groups, take advantage of the tools your conference platform provides, or research the ever-expanding list of free or inexpensive tools for activities, such as:

- brainstorming
- mind mapping
- decision making
- document editing
- task and project management
- providing feedback
- time tracking
- status updates
- collaboration via touch screens
- remote working retreats.

You can list categories of tools to facilitate idea generation, problem definition, problem analysis, and decision making (Tool 4-1). The sections that follow detail each technique and the guidelines for implementing them.

## TOOL 4-1
### FACILITATOR TOOLS BY PROCESS STEP

| Process | Tools |
|---------|-------|
| Identifying and generating ideas | Round robins<br>Anonymous suggestions<br>Brainwriting<br>Mind mapping<br>Reverse brainstorming |
| Defining and analyzing problems | Mind mapping<br>Fish bone diagramming<br>Storyboarding<br>SCAMPER<br>Six Thinking Hats |
| Listing and prioritizing solutions | Affinity diagrams<br>Multivoting or nominal group technique<br>Spectrum listening |

| Process | Tools |
|---|---|
| Decision making | Classic group problem-solving method |
| | Force-field analyses |
| | Voting |
| | Dots |
| | Consensus cards |
| | Matrices and decision tables |

# Facilitation Tools for Idea Generation, Analysis, and Problem Solving

Not all groups are naturally creative. In fact, groups can actually stifle individual creativity due to "group think," the fear of being criticized or mocked, and the inefficiency of one person offering an idea, having the group respond, and then repeating. According to research by Andre P. Walton and Markus Kemmelmeier (2012), organizational cultures that promote "collective norms" over "individual norms"—in other words, that strive for the benefit of the company as a whole rather than individual successes—tend to be less creative. And, ironically, tight-knit teams that tend to work frequently and well together "can be a double-edged sword, as it may undermine creativity." An effective facilitator will use idea-generating techniques to help even the most analytical of teams or the most familiar of teams think outside the box. Remind participants of idea-generating ground rules prior to beginning any creative session:

- No criticism of an idea is allowed.
- Strive for the longest list possible. Go for quantity of ideas; you can trim the list down to the top few later.
- Strive for creativity—wild and crazy ideas are encouraged!
- Build on the ideas of others— "hitchhike" or "piggyback."

## POINTER

A number of factors influence how much and at what level people participate in team meetings, such as:
- level of self-confidence
- knowledge of the topic
- degree of familiarity with others in the group
- level in the organization.

For groups with particularly dominant or quiet individuals, consider techniques that promote relatively equal participation among all group members.

Consider the following idea-generation methods and adapt for your group as necessary. Don't forget to take advantage of other well-known idea-generating activities as well, including brainstorming, pros and cons lists, and SWOT analyses (listing strengths, weaknesses, opportunities, and threats of a situation). For virtual meetings, use tools such as virtual whiteboards, chat, and breakout rooms for these idea-generating activities.

## Round-Robins

Round-robins encourage relatively equal participation among all group members. In this activity, the facilitator asks each person to state one idea pertinent to the question posed.

1. Pose a question to the group.
2. Give individuals in the group time to ponder the question and generate at least one idea. Stress that they may want to come up with several ideas in case there are duplicates. The goal is to generate new ideas.
3. Call time.
4. Either ask for a volunteer or call on one person to state their idea, which is recorded on a whiteboard or flipchart.
5. Go to the next group member and continue the process of asking for ideas and posting them. If any members have more than one idea, they need to wait until their next turn to express each idea.
6. Continue the round-robin until all ideas have been stated.

## Anonymous Suggestions

In some situations, people may be reluctant to express their ideas aloud. For example, in a meeting with participants from all hierarchical levels in the organization, certain people may be intimidated, fearful that those higher in the chain of command will judge their ideas negatively. Or, if the topic is particularly sensitive, participants may be reluctant to express their views or ideas publicly. Anonymity may loosen them up.

1. Pose a question to the group.
2. Give individuals in the group time to ponder the question and generate at least one idea. Instruct participants to anonymously jot down their ideas on paper, index cards, or sticky notes.
3. Call time.
4. Collect the cards and read them to the group. The goal is for anonymity to help the group get more creative with their ideas and generate a greater number of ideas without fear of repercussions holding them back.

## Brainwriting

This technique generates a large number of ideas or solutions. The underlying principle is that the greater number of ideas the team generates, the greater the possibility that it will identify a quality solution. This approach enables participants to benefit from the ideas of others and to generate new ideas.

1. Break the group into teams of four to six members.
2. Pose a question or problem. Direct participants to individually come up with as many solutions as possible and to write them on paper. No discussion is allowed.
3. Call time.
4. Ask the participants to pass their responses to someone else in their group (for example, everyone pass to the right) or to place their papers in the middle of the table and exchange them for someone else's.
5. Instruct the individuals to use the lists they now hold as inspiration to try to generate additional ideas or modifications.
6. Continue to exchange, still in silence, until the agreed-upon time limit is reached.
7. Collect the papers. Review and evaluate the ideas at a later time.

## Mind Mapping

This technique is also called idea mapping, clustering, webbing, or spidering. It is a fast, fun method of free association that produces ideas. It helps members suspend judgment of ideas and can be used either individually or in a group. An example of mind mapping is given in Tool 4-2.

## TOOL 4-2
## MIND MAPPING EXAMPLE

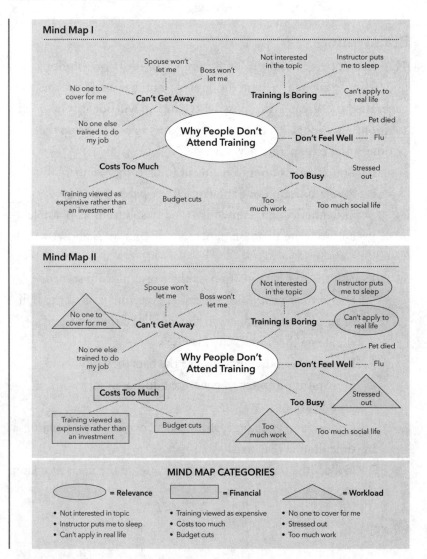

1. Instruct participants to write a word or phrase on a piece of paper that describes the problem.
2. Draw a circle around the problem statement.
3. For two minutes, write down all aspects of the problem.
4. Connect the related words with arrows or lines.
5. Look for three or four main themes or categories and assign a geometric symbol (for example, a square, circle, triangle, diamond) to each category.
6. Discuss the findings.

## Fishbone Diagramming

Sometimes stating the problem and clarifying it in a brief discussion is sufficient. Often, however, this is not enough, and you need more formal techniques to help the group work toward an understanding of the problem. One helpful technique is called a fishbone diagram— also known as an Ishikawa diagram or cause-and-effect diagram.

Fishbone diagrams emerged from the practice of quality assurance as a way of graphically identifying the factors affecting quality. In this context, facilitators use it as a way of identifying specifics that influence the desired outcome. For example, a group of executives looking at declining sales might incorrectly (or prematurely) conclude that the decline results from inadequate marketing. Rather than jumping to conclusions, the group could use a fishbone diagram to examine the range of factors that might be causing the problem (Tool 4-3).

1. The group lists any and all factors related to the question or problem posed.
2. The group places the factors into categories, such as environment, time, resources, people, and so on.
3. The group begins to fill in the diagram.

Each major branch represents one of the categories of factors. The steps connected to the branch represent the more particular items from the original list. As the diagram grows, additional ideas emerge, and the group adds them to the diagram.

What frequently happens is that one or two branches receives more attention than the others, and the group has an "aha" experience.

Participants see the problem in a different light because of the diagram's ability to illuminate patterns.

## TOOL 4-3
### FISHBONE DIAGRAM EXAMPLE

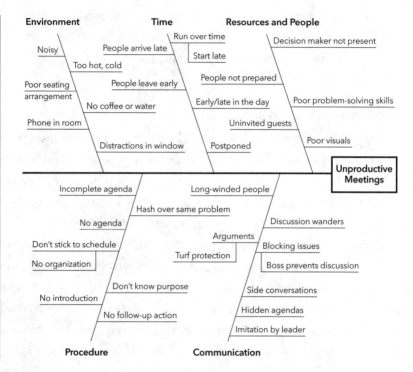

## Affinity Diagramming

Affinity diagrams (also referred to as affinity maps or groups) gather a large number of ideas, organize these ideas into logical groupings based on the natural relationships between items, and define groups of items. A follow-up to the affinity diagram is the interrelationship diagram, which charts cause-and-effect relationships among the groupings. They are best used with complex issues when relationships among facts seem confusing, when thoughts or facts are ambiguous or disorganized, or when the group needs to discover the major themes contained in a great number of ideas (Tool 4-4).

# TOOL 4-4
## AFFINITY DIAGRAM EXAMPLE

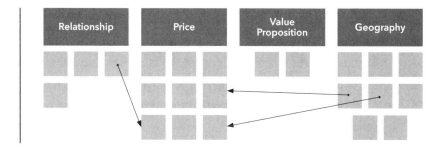

Write the question or problem on a flipchart or whiteboard.

1. Working silently, each individual records their ideas in response to the question on sticky notes (one idea per note). The group members hold all ideas until the next step.

2. Place notes on a specified surface. Without discussing their ideas, team members move to a specially prepared wall (covered with flipchart or butcher paper) or another flat surface and place the completed notes randomly on the prepared surface.

3. Sort ideas into related groups. When all of the notes are placed on the surface, the group members, working in silence and moving quickly, use their "gut reactions" to move notes into related groups. Individuals can move any note anywhere on the surface. Disputes or disagreements about placement of notes are resolved silently. After an interval, the group is allowed to discuss their notes and finalize the groupings.

4. Create the category title. When all ideas are located in a category of related ideas, the group identifies the one idea or note that captures the essence of all the ideas in that group. This category title is written on the surface, and lines are drawn to enclose all ideas related to that title.

---

5. Next, the group looks for interrelationships among the categories. This step in the process involves looking at each category and comparing it to other categories and then asking the questions, "What is the relationship between these two? Which category causes or influences the rest?" If a relationship exists between two categories, the group draws a line that links the categories and notes the direction of the cause-and-effect relationship with an arrow.

6. Identify the key drivers. The last step in the interrelationship diagram involves identifying the categories that are the primary drivers or influencers. For each category, total up the number of outgoing and incoming arrows and write the totals next to each category. The categories with the greatest influence—the primary drivers or causes—are those with the most outgoing arrows. Those with the most incoming arrows tend to be the results or effects of other forces on the page and therefore not a high-leverage choice for affecting change in the outcomes. The purpose of this activity is to focus on the factors that have the greatest influence on the issue.

The outcomes of affinity and interrelationship diagrams are large groups of ideas that are categorized into related clusters of ideas, each with a clear title, and with the relationships clearly drawn. Furthermore, the key drivers or influencers are identified as a first step in developing a high-leverage strategy for causing lasting change in the system.

## Multivoting (Nominal Group Technique)

Multivoting, or nominal group technique, is a structured method that a team can use to brainstorm a wide range of responses to an issue, clarify each of the responses, and rank the responses from most to least important. Facilitators often use this technique with a team of representative stakeholders to minimize the impact of team dynamics in generating, evaluating, and ranking or selecting solutions.

1. Write the question or problem on a flipchart or whiteboard. Ensure that everyone understands the issue.
2. Ask each team member to develop a written list of ideas or suggestions. This is done individually, privately, and silently. Note that team members should record all their ideas, rejecting none.
3. After lists are complete, ask each participant—in a round-robin fashion—to offer one idea from their list. As each person responds, record the idea on a flipchart and number each item. Individuals may skip ideas already offered by someone else. Continue in rounds until the team has offered all its ideas.
4. After all ideas are recorded, lead the group in clarifying, linking, discussing, or eliminating ideas. Make notations on the flipchart to help improve the understanding of each idea. The goal of this step is to reduce the list to a single roster of distinct, well-defined ideas.
5. Participants review the list and select their top five priority items. Each member notes on paper ballots the number of the item and a word or phrase that describes the item (one item per ballot). Then each team member ranks the ballots from five (most important) to one (least important).
6. The team gives its ballots to the facilitator who records the rankings (five through one) from the ballots on the flipchart pages next to the item receiving a vote.
7. Total the points for each item. The item that receives the most points is ranked most important by the entire group.

The outcome of multivoting is a rank-ordered list of items—each clearly defined and understood by group members.

## Spectrum Listening

This technique provides a mechanism for analyzing the major advantages and blocks to the group's ideas and suggestions. Rather than viewing the ideas as good or bad, spectrum listening encourages

STEP 4

participants to hear and evaluate each idea thoroughly by listening for, and making statements about, three key areas.

1. Have a participant present an idea.
2. Ask the group to listen for and make statements about:
   - what they like about the idea
   - what concerns they have about the idea
   - how their concerns can be turned into opportunities.
3. Discuss and evaluate the idea.

## Reverse Brainstorming

Reverse brainstorming helps to spark creativity when a group is stumped for ideas. To use this technique, begin by posing your question or problem in reverse. For example, rather than, "How can we decrease accidents in our factory?" ask, "How can we increase accidents in our factory?" Ideas and solutions can then be reversed, hopefully producing some real answers.

1. Clearly identify the problem or question and write it down.
2. Reverse the problem or question.
3. Brainstorm the reverse problem to generate reverse solution ideas.
4. Once you have brainstormed all the ideas to solve the reverse problem, now reverse these into solutions for the original problem or challenge.

## POINTER

Collaborative activities like brainstorming and discussions help promote a deeper understanding of the problems and potential solutions. The act of articulating one's own ideas aloud fosters deeper psychological processing, as opposed to just listening or reading.

## Storyboarding

A storyboard helps to organize thoughts visually and is especially helpful when trying to generate ideas for a process or solving a problem that is part of a process. By examining the process visually, the group will be able to see how ideas connect, identify any missing pieces of the process, or spot opportunities for improvement. Tool 4-5 illustrates a sample storyboard.

## TOOL 4-5
### STORYBOARD DIAGRAM EXAMPLE

Question: How can we reduce the customer delivery time?

| Scene: | Scene: | Scene: |
|---|---|---|
| Customer places order. | Sales sends technical specifications to manufacturing plant. | Manufacturing approves specifications. |

| Scene: | Scene: | Scene: |
|---|---|---|
| Manufacturing produces products. | Warehouse receives products and ships to customer. | Customer receives and inspects products. |

1. Start by stating the problem or question.
2. Give group members a few minutes to consider the steps leading up to the problem, and what happens after the problem. Have them write down their ideas.
3. Have the storyboard diagram posted for everyone to see, either on a whiteboard or flipchart or projected on a screen. As a group, discuss how to fill in the boxes with the steps leading up to the problem and what happens after the problem.
4. Look for patterns and relationships in the steps and try to find the story. What are the missing pieces? How can the process be improved?

## SCAMPER

SCAMPER (Substitute, Combine, Adapt, Modify, Put to another use, Eliminate, Reverse) is designed to improve or alter an existing idea, for example an existing product or service. This technique helps the group to see the problem and possible solutions from different angles. For each letter, ask the group a question about the problem that you are trying to solve.

1. On a whiteboard or flipchart, write the following words and phrase: Substitute, Combine, Adapt, Modify, Put to another use, Eliminate, Reverse. (You may want to use one page of a flipchart for each one.)

2. Ask the group the following questions, moving through the letters of SCAMPER. Record their answers on the flipchart or whiteboard (or ask a volunteer to write the answers as you facilitate the discussions). Alter the questions to fit your problem and your group.

   ◦ **Substitute**—What would happen to the project if we swapped X for Y? What resources or materials can we swap or substitute to enhance the product? Which rules can we substitute or change? Is it possible to replace someone involved?

   ◦ **Combine**—What would happen to the project if we combined X and Y? What parts or concepts could be combined? Can we combine two existing products to create something new? Can we combine the objectives or purposes of two existing products or services to create something new? How can we combine resources or talent to develop a new way of thinking about this product?

   ◦ **Adapt**—Is there a solution to a similar problem that we can adapt for this problem? Are there solutions outside of our industry that we can apply?

   ◦ **Modify**—What could we modify to create more value on this project? What can we modify to make the product stronger or less vulnerable to competition? Can we modify any of the processes related to this product?

- **Put to another use**—What other uses or applications might this project have? Is it possible to utilize this product elsewhere, maybe in another industry? Who else can utilize this product? Someone older or younger? Where else can this product be used?

- **Eliminate**—What could we remove from the project to simplify it? Can we break this into smaller parts? What part of the process can we eliminate? Are there any rules regarding this product we can eliminate? How can we minimize cost, effort, or time?

- **Reverse**—How could we reorganize this problem to make it more effective? Can we change the order of the process? Can we reverse the roles of any of the people? (For example, can we ask quality control personnel to check the product before the line manager makes their final inspection?) How can we accomplish the opposite effect?

3. After moving through the letters of SCAMPER, reflect on the group's answers and see if any potential solutions have been uncovered. Help the group synthesize the stronger ideas and create next steps.

## Six Thinking Hats

Six Thinking Hats is a system designed by psychologist Edward de Bono that allows individuals within a group to consider specific priorities and perspectives. This technique allows groups to explore a problem from six different angles.

1. The "hats" can be worn in several different ways. Select which will work best for your group:

- If the group is large enough for six different teams, you can divide participants into teams of two to five people and the entire team wears one hat.

- For smaller groups, appoint one person to wear each hat.

2. Assign hats to the various teams or participants, based on the descriptions below:
   - **White Hat**—This person considers just the facts.
   - **Yellow Hat**—This is the optimist of the group, looking for benefits of the idea.
   - **Black Hat**—The devil's advocate, this person's role is to look for potential obstacles and dangers.
   - **Red Hat**—This person discusses their gut feelings and hunches; no reasons need to be given.
   - **Green Hat**—This is the creative role, considering new ideas and innovative solutions to any obstacles raised by the Black Hat.
   - **Blue Hat**—This person takes on the role of facilitator within this group, ensuring the rules of the exercise are followed.

3. Give the participants several minutes to consider the problem from their assigned perspectives. Have them write down their ideas and suggestions.

4. Call time.

5. Go around the room and discuss the ideas and suggestions from one perspective at a time. Post ideas where visible for all and discuss, trying to eventually arrive at a viable solution.

## Facilitation Tools for Making Decisions

Groups are notoriously inefficient at making decisions, even once they generate ideas to solve problem. Organizations often convene work groups to complete inherently complex, novel, or territorially volatile tasks—with no problem-solving method to follow. Or individual group members become wedded to particular ideas and thus muddy the decision-making process by failing to let go if the rest of the group isn't in agreement.

Teams should not only have a method and tools to help make decisions, but they should also agree early in the meeting—before they get stuck—to use a particular method.

You can begin with the classic group problem-solving method, and then add on the tools and techniques that follow as necessary to enhance and customize the process.

The classic group problem-solving technique is an analytical approach that can be applied to any problem and is useful when helping a group make critical or formal decisions. It helps ensure everyone has a clear and consistent understanding of the problem before solutions are discussed. Depending on the size of your group and the length of discussion time, estimate at least one hour to move through this process.

**Step One:** Define the problem. Simply stated, a problem is a discrepancy between what is and what should be. One of the advantages of a group is that its members have widely different perspectives and their understanding of the problem can vary significantly. If not adequately managed, however, this advantage can become a disadvantage. At this stage, the group should:

**POINTER**

Successful facilitators select suitable decision-making strategies based on an assessment of the problem the group faces. Consider whether the group is trying to generate ideas, evaluate ideas, or come to agreement on the best solution.

- Be explicit about the language used and what it means. Participants should provide specific descriptions and examples. Make sure to ask the group frequently if any clarification is needed around any point.
- Question assumptions and perceptions.
- Make comparisons between the situation now versus the way the group would like it to be. How long has the problem existed? Who is affected? What obstacles are in the way of the desired result?

This step of defining the problem is often overlooked in the process. It's a critical step, however, because the effectiveness of the rest of the process requires all participants to have a clear, common understanding—and to express that in commonly understood language.

For example, imagine you are facilitating a group of environmentalists and commercial developers addressing land-use policy in a wilderness area. Each subgroup emotionally argues its position for and against a change in policy until you press the subgroups for a definition of "wilderness." Each has a different operational interpretation of the term. When they come to a common understanding of the term, many of the apparently unmanageable differences evaporate.

The goal for this stage of the process is for the group to compose a problem statement: one sentence that summarizes the problem. For example, "Our manufacturing plant has made 20 percent more mistakes this year than last year."

Be careful to not suggest a solution in the problem statement. Ensure everyone agrees on the problem statement and clearly understands it before moving on.

## POINTER

Be explicit about the language used and what it means. Make participants provide specific descriptions and examples to ensure that everyone is using apples-to-apples definitions, and all are on the same page.

**Step Two:** Research and analyze the problem. If the prior stage focused on *what* the problem is, this stage of the process asks the participants to establish *why* the problem is happening.

Questions to consider:
- What are the root causes of the problem? Why is it happening now?
- What issues related to this problem are urgent? What issues are important but can be accomplished as a long-term goal?

If possible, plan to have any relevant research available to the group for this stage. This research could be assigned before the meeting as pre-work; or, give the group time and access to resources to research relevant data. As new data emerge, it is common to see the problem redefined.

**Step Three:** Establish criteria and generate possible solutions. We all make rational decisions by evaluating options using one or more criteria. Frequently, however, criteria are not made explicit, so the reasons an individual has for preferring one option to another remain hidden from the group members. The consequence is that the group perceives this person's preference as somewhat irrational.

For a group to succeed in making decisions, group members must make public and explicit the criteria that are important to them. And because all criteria are not equal, you also need to determine the relative importance or weight of each criterion. For example, criteria may include:

- The solution must be within a certain budget.
- The solution must be done with internal resources only.
- The solution must be implemented within eight weeks.
- The solution must be kept confidential, especially to competitors.

Once the group has settled on criteria, use one of the idea-generating techniques in this step to brainstorm possible solutions. Teams often begin the process with this step; however, resist that temptation. Make sure the group has a clear understanding of the problem, has researched contributing factors, and has established solution criteria first.

Only then is it time to put the thinking caps on and generate a variety of ideas. Encourage the group to consider all possible options. Don't evaluate the ideas too closely yet; go for quantity. Your goal at this point is to understand what you *could* do to solve this problem, not what you *should* do.

Again, ensure participants understand each other well. Encourage group members to ask questions like, "Could you please explain your reasoning more?" or "Could you clarify that point for me with an example?"

If the group becomes really stuck, you may have to return to the first step and better define the problem. Or, you may have to break the problem into several components and brainstorm solutions for each component separately.

**Step Four:** Evaluate solutions. This stage involves systematically assessing each viable option against the criteria and choosing the "best" options (that is, the ones that stack up best against the criteria).

Verify that everyone understands each idea or solution. This is also the appropriate point in the process for the group to become critical about the ideas generated. At this step, help the group clarify discussions, summarize the results of their process of evaluating and narrowing solutions, keep the group on track, and help reach consensus so that everyone buys in to the final decision.

**Step Five:** Choose the best solution. As the group narrows the list of solutions, help them reach a final decision by majority vote, by weighing the pros and cons, or by discussing them until a consensus is reached.

As a group begins to settle on one solution, ask: Can this solution be improved? Does this solution live up to the purpose of this group? Also ask the group about any unintended negative consequences of this solution.

Be careful that participants don't settle too soon—that they don't choose a solution that seems to solve the problem without continuing to look for a better solution. Although one solution may be adequate, superior solutions stem from divergent thinking—creatively exploring possible solutions before agreeing on any one choice. There are two types of solutions:

- solutions that are mutually exclusive
- solutions that can be combined.

Too often, groups treat solutions as "either/or," rather than "both/and," which results in unnecessary polarization when they might be able to compromise.

Consider the following decision-making techniques to help with your group.

## Voting

Voting is a commonly used decision-making method. Although it helps the group to arrive at a quick decision, voting results in winners and losers. When the group votes, a successful facilitator helps the meeting participants let go of personal attachments and realize decisions are being made for the organization's benefit, not their own.

There are several types of voting in which each person has one vote, including:

- Simple majority—The decision is made when more than half of the group chooses the same solution.
- Super majority—The decision is made when two-thirds of the group agrees to the same solution.

You can use one of these voting measurements, or any other one that suits the group and their objectives.

## Force-Field Analyses

Kurt Lewin (1890–1947)—sometimes called the grandfather of organization development because of his profound effect on the field—defined two factors that influence change in organizations: driving and restraining forces. These forces either work for or against a particular change. The goal is to maximize positive change forces, known as "driving forces," and to minimize or eliminate the negative ones, known as "restraining forces." Facilitators use force-field analysis to encourage driving forces and discourage restraining forces (Tool 4-6).

## TOOL 4-6
### DRIVING AND RESTRAINING FORCES

| Driving Forces | Restraining Forces |
|---|---|
| Factors that work toward our goal | Factors that work against our goal |
|  |  |
|  |  |

1. Create and display the group's goal statement of what needs to be achieved in the chart.
2. Brainstorm ideas.
3. Help the group gain agreement on the specific driving and restraining factors that move the group toward the desired goal.

4. After compiling a list of ideas for both sides of the chart, work with the group to agree on the two or three driving forces to maximize, as well as two or three restraining forces to minimize.
5. Brainstorm and list the steps for the actions required to strengthen or decrease the forces identified.

## Dots

This is a simple and time-efficient method for voting on ideas or solutions. It ensures that all members are actively involved, and it presents a visual representation of areas of consensus.

1. List all the previously generated ideas on a flipchart or large sheets of paper.
2. Give each participant an allotment of self-adhesive, colored dots, or give each participant a unique pen or pencil color.
3. Instruct participants to vote for ideas by placing a colored dot next to each idea. Dots can be allocated in any manner. For example, if each person is given 10 dots, all of the dots may be placed next to one idea, or three dots may be placed next to one idea and seven dots placed next to another.
4. Tally the votes. The ideas with the greatest number of votes are selected for further analysis or implementation.

## Consensus Cards

For this technique, group members use red, yellow, or green cards to show their position on an issue at any point during the discussion. The consensus cards can be made of colored construction paper, or paper with red, yellow, or green dots drawn with a marker or highlighter. Tape three cards (one of each color) together to form a three-sided tent. Red means "I disagree," yellow means "I can live with the decision," and green indicates "I agree." When all participants have shown the card with the same color, either red, yellow, or green, they have reached a consensus.

1. Define the issue or problem.
2. Instruct the participants to place the yellow face of their card tent toward the center of the table.
3. Discuss the solutions. When asked, the participants may change the color of their card tent that is facing the center of the table to indicate their position on the topic.
4. Discussion stops when all are in agreement (that is, all tents have the same color cards showing).

## Matrices (Weighted Decision Tables)

Matrices, or weighted decision tables, help evaluate solutions against predetermined criteria. A major advantage of this method is that it recognizes the relative importance of each criterion (Tool 4-7).

STEP 4

## TOOL 4-7
## SAMPLE MATRIX: SITE SELECTION

| Criteria | Availability of Parking | Proximity to Public Transportation | Rental Fee | Capacity to Accommodate a Large Group | Total |
|---|---|---|---|---|---|
| Criteria Rating | 5 | 5 | 7 | 3 | |
| Site A | 4 / 20 | 1 / 5 | 3 / 21 | 7 / 21 | 67 |
| Site B | 5 / 25 | 6 / 30 | 3 / 21 | 5 / 15 | 91 |
| Site C | 3 / 15 | 5 / 25 | 2 / 14 | 6 / 18 | 70 |

*Used with permission from Darraugh (1997).*

1. On a whiteboard or flipchart, write the problem and list the known solutions.
2. Brainstorm the decision criteria.
3. Evaluate the decision criteria and determine the importance of each item.

4. Construct a matrix table (see Tool 4-6 for an example).

5. List the criteria across the top and the potential solutions down the left side of the matrix.

6. Using a scale of one to seven, with one being low importance and seven being high importance, ask the group to assign a value to each criterion. Record that rating in the row below each criterion.

7. Using the same rating scale, ask the team to rate each idea against each criterion. Record the rating in the upper portion of the diagonal line.

8. Multiply the rating for each idea by the weight given to each criterion, and write the product in the lower portion of the diagonal line.

9. Add the products for each idea and write the sum in the total score column.

10. The idea with the highest total score is the group's choice.

No matter which facilitation tool or technique is selected, the most successful facilitators focus on improving group decision making by attending to the following technical issues:

- applying structure
- making roles explicit
- using ground rules
- exploring the problems systematically
- using models to evaluate options.

Concentrating on structure does not deny the interpersonal dimension of human decision making. It does, however, help to minimize the unhealthy aspects of emotion that can emerge in the process.

Successful facilitators select suitable decision-making strategies based on an assessment of the problem the group faces. Combined with good meeting protocol, such as adhering to an agenda, facilitators elicit both effectiveness and efficiency in the group's interactions.

## The Next Step

Now that basic techniques to facilitate a work group session have been selected, the next step requires facilitators to determine which media and technology to use for greatest impact and achievement of goals.

# Step 5

# Integrate Media and Technology for Impact

## Overview

- Determine which visual aids meet your needs.
- Select appropriate media.
- Master different types of visual aids.

Chances are you'll use at least one type of media to help guide and support the facilitation process. In fact, selecting the media to use is one of the most significant decisions that you will make. Keep in mind that the media selected must support the session goals and facilitation process. Don't treat the facilitation of a meeting as an opportunity to show off the company's shiny new toy.

Visual aids can help to make bland, passive sessions come to life by getting participants up and moving around as they brainstorm ideas on flipcharts or whiteboards. Presentation software can help to illustrate background information such as process flows and organizational levels.

Because many people have an easier time remembering something they have seen than something they have heard, most facilitation sessions benefit from some use of visual media. However, it is important to plan and prepare visual aids to support the facilitation process rather than distract from it. You should carefully prepare all visuals and materials ahead of time, reviewing them for typos and good design as well as other considerations, to reflect professionalism and to convey respect for the group or the client organization.

Aside from helping a group to understand issues, visual aids:

- Promote clarity, capture ideas, organize and summarize rationale, and facilitate decision making.
- Assist with the flow and structure of the information to maintain the audience's attention as you reveal the key points and follow a logical decision-making process.
- Enable the participants to see what something looks like, clarify relationships among numerical data, and understand the organizational structure of information.

So which visual aid should you use based on the type of session you need to facilitate?

## Determine the Needs of the Meeting

There are many types of visual aids to choose from when planning the facilitation session: whiteboards, posters, flipcharts, presentation software, or streaming media, to name a few. There are advantages and disadvantages to each visual aid, and some lend themselves better to specific circumstances than others. Which type of visual aid you choose will depend on the facilitation goals, the makeup of the group, and your budget. The following questions will help you to select the appropriate visual aid.

- What do you know about the audience (perhaps from their audience profile) and their expectations for the facilitation session? You need to ensure that materials and activities are informative and support the process, but do not confuse or overwhelm the participants.
- Will sound, motion, color, or other effects be required to communicate the message effectively? Would a demonstration help the audience understand a concept (especially for technical problems)? If you only need to highlight specific points, text slides might be sufficient.

- Under what conditions is the facilitation session taking place? What will be the room size, the size of the group, and the availability of equipment and other media?
- Do you have the resources—time, money, expertise, and support—to develop appropriate visual aids to their best advantage?

## Select Appropriate Media

Keep in mind that the size of the room, the setup, and how it supports or hinders movement will dictate the appropriate media for a facilitation session. Media must support the desired level of movement. For example, groups and breakout sessions encourage participants to be active and move around. But media often tie participants to their seats, at least for that portion of the meeting.

Your choice of media should also depend on the time of day and the types of activities you plan. For example, media with higher levels of interaction are great for the period right after lunch, at the end of the day, or if participants have been sitting passively for a while. Use Tool 5-1 to determine which type of media are appropriate based on their ability to support higher and lower interactivity.

## TOOL 5-1
### INTERACTIVITY LEVELS ASSOCIATED WITH DIFFERENT MEDIA

| Media With Higher Interactivity | Media With Lower Interactivity |
| --- | --- |
| Handouts with blanks to be filled in | Handouts with all text filled in |
| Whiteboards and flipcharts that participants create themselves | Whiteboards and flipcharts that the facilitator fills in |
| Physical props that participants can examine and handle | Physical props that only the facilitator handles |
| Walls, flipcharts, or whiteboards that participants post sticky notes on | Streaming video |
|  | Presentation software slides |

## Master Different Types of Visual Aids

Facilitators can utilize myriad visual aids to conduct an effective and engaging meeting. For example, flipcharts and whiteboards enable people to draw and write information on the fly. Presentation software enables you to create formal, structured, professional-looking presentations. Streaming media can share examples of situations that are impossible to recreate in the meeting room. But not all of these options are appropriate all of the time. In order to determine which ones will best enhance the meeting you facilitate, you should understand the advantages and best uses of each one. The following are the most common and versatile visual aids you may use.

### Flipcharts

A flipchart is a low-tech visual aid usually consisting of an easel and large pads of paper. You can purchase a variety of flipchart paper—including some with adhesive on the backs that can be displayed around the room, like large sticky notes. Other varieties of flipchart paper include blank pages, lined pages, or even grids. Flipcharts are a great resource for smaller group meetings and facilitation sessions, especially for capturing key points from brainstorming sessions or when a concept is easier to illustrate than describe.

When working with a flipchart, stand to one side. Which side you stand on depends on which hand you write with. For example, if you are right-handed, stand on the left side of the flipchart (from the participants' point of view). If you are using tabs to help you navigate the flipchart pages, position the tabs on the left side as well (again, as the participants see the chart). If you are left-handed, then reverse this stance and placement.

So that you remember to talk to the group and not your flipchart, touch the paper when you're writing on it, turn to face your audience, and then talk to them about what you've written. If you see group members craning their necks to see the flipchart, that is your cue to move or to position the flipchart so that everyone can see it more readily.

As a guideline, use flipcharts in the following situations:

- **When you want to capture participant ideas and comments**—Most facilitators can create professional-looking flipcharts by hand (if you have good hand writing) with little effort. For example, use flipcharts during project team meetings to list the top project issues or to capture ideas in a brainstorming session.

- **When the audience and room size are appropriate**—Flipcharts are ideal in rooms with 30 or fewer participants when they are positioned so that everyone has a good line of sight. They provide a central place to capture ideas and questions generated during the session.

- **When the meeting is in the afternoon**— Flipcharts are especially helpful for meetings conducted immediately after lunch or in the late afternoon because you do not need to dim the lights as you would for a slide presentation.

- **When you have little or no budget**— Flipcharts are a perfect choice when a last-minute meeting has made its way onto your calendar and you have little time or budget to prepare a formal

**POINTER**

Flipcharts—one of a facilitator's best tools—should be leveraged extensively to post the agenda, capture parking-lot items, diagram problems or issues, post brainstorm ideas, and rank or weight solutions to determine a few viable options.

presentation with slides or other media. With flipcharts, you can create the key points, graphs, charts, or other information to facilitate a meeting almost anytime, anywhere, and on a limited budget.

- **When you need to use a flipchart as support**—Because flipcharts can be created in advance, many facilitators also use them as a personal support tool (or a cheat sheet) as a quick reminder of the topics and activities coming up. Another trick is to write in pencil on the corners of blank

## POINTER

Consider these 10 simple rules when creating flipcharts:

- Use a maximum of six lines per page; busy flipcharts obscure your message.
- Use only eight to 10 words per point, and use key words or phrases instead of full sentences.
- Verify that the participants can easily read the information from all areas of the room.
- Use headings on each page to orient the group to the ideas generated, points discussed, and so on.
- Use three to four different colors to make text and drawings eye-catching and easy to read, but make sure the colors are easy for participants to see.
- If you tape flipchart pages to a wall, leave a blank page behind to ensure that the marker won't bleed through the paper onto the wall.
- Lightly, in pencil, in the top corner of each page, write a brief heading of what's on the next page to help you segue seamlessly to the topics to cover next or material on the following page.
- Number each page of your flipchart, then mark the corresponding number in your facilitator notes to help you quickly get back on track if you get distracted or lose your place.
- Always check the spelling of your flipcharts.
- Use sticky notes, sticky tabs, or clear tape to form tabs at the side of each sheet so that you can quickly navigate to the specific page you want.

flipchart pages so that only the facilitator can see the information. This enables facilitators to appear as though they are posing off-the-cuff questions to the group when in fact the sequence of the session and the specific questions asked have been carefully planned.

- **When you want to display a visual during the entire meeting**—Flipcharts are particularly effective when you want to display a visual, graph, or statement during the entire session to reference from time to time.

Despite these great advantages, flipcharts are not a good idea if your handwriting is barely legible. To increase your legibility, try printing in block letters using flipchart paper with lines or a grid. If the audience still can't read your writing, you may want to try a different visual aid.

## Presentation Software

PowerPoint, the most well-known type of presentation software, is a popular visual aid. Where overhead projectors and transparencies were once a staple of meetings, today presentation software now reigns as king of communication aids in many organizations. But it's important to note that PowerPoint is not the only presentation software. Many others are gaining traction, including Prezi, WPS Office Free, LibreOffice, Canva, and iCloud Keynote. Each requires practice to master, and each can bring new creativity and impressive visuals to your audience.

Whichever software you choose, you'll need to project the slides for your audience to see. You can do this in several ways, depending on the size of your group:

- a laptop computer or display monitor for small groups
- a digital projector that interfaces directly with a laptop
- a computer projector that sends images directly from your monitor onto a screen or flat surface—this is used for larger groups
- in-ceiling projector screens
- hard copies of slides that can be distributed as handouts.

STEP 5

Presentation software offers many advantages over traditional visual aids; for example, its ease of use and the ability to capture facilitator's notes on each slide, hidden from the rest of the audience. This allows you to either print your key talking points, which shows the slide image and your speaking notes, or display your speaking notes on the slide on your own computer while projecting only the slide itself to the rest of the participants.

## POINTER

Here are 10 rules to apply when using presentation software:
- Keep the design clean.
- Don't add too many effects or use too many different fonts.
- Keep the background subtle.
- Use clip art sparingly.
- Use the most appropriate graph style for the data you share.
- Limit colors to three per slide.
- Adhere to the six-by-six format: No more than six words per line and no more than six lines per slide.
- Use light colors on dark backgrounds.
- Keep sound and music clips brief.
- Check for projection quality before the session begins.

As a guideline, use presentation software when:

- **Your meeting is formal**—Presentation software tools are not only easy to use, but they also enable you to produce high-quality, professional-looking presentations.

- **You need flexibility to modify the meeting materials**— Presentation software enables you to quickly add or replace slides using your laptop. You can easily tweak the topics and agenda and rearrange the flow of activities to support the group's priorities.

- **You need a visual aid appropriate for audiences of all sizes**— Materials created using this tool are just as appropriate for one or two people sitting around a table or for a large group in a conference center.

- **You want to reveal information in a specific manner**—When conducting a facilitation session, presentation software is especially adept at helping you to reveal the information that you want, when you want, to guide the group through a logical problem-identification and decision-making process. Presentation software includes "builds" where you successively reveal points or information from a complete slide with a click or motion of the mouse, in addition to displaying all the content at once. This feature can even dim the previous topics to help orient the participants to the current topic of discussion, while leaving previous content displayed for context, in case they become distracted during the meeting.

With all these advantages of presentation software, is there ever a time when you should not use this tool? As a general rule, do not use presentation software when:

- **It might become a crutch**—Presentation software puts the focus on the slides, rather than the audience. It's a great tool, but it can quickly turn a facilitation session into a presentation. You've heard of death by PowerPoint, where teams are slowly bored to tears as the presenter talks through one slide after another. If you feel you may unintentionally allow this to happen, choose other ways to present material, like flipcharts or even a video that has an obvious end point.
- **You haven't practiced the software**—You might want to avoid using presentation software unless you have adequate time to practice using the tool. If you are not familiar with the tool you might find yourself focusing more on pressing the right buttons than on facilitating discussions.

## Streaming Media and Live Internet

Using informational videos or even live video feeds can be an effective part of a facilitation session as a means of conveying a concept, providing background information, or simply offering some entertainment or a catalyst for discussion. These visual aids are particularly effective for demonstrating desired skills, behavior, and processes. For example, a five-minute movie clip of the Apollo 13 team in Houston solving problems with limited tools might segue into a discussion about creativity within constraints.

When arranging and checking the meeting location setup, make sure that the proper equipment is available and working, and you know how to use it, especially an Internet connection that can support streaming media. Make sure the sound is loud enough to be heard through the room. Even it's a small group and you plan to stream just using your laptop, bring speakers to amplify the sound. While mishaps happen to everyone on occasion, having to apologize for equipment failures or your lack of expertise is a great way to undermine your credibility as the facilitator. After all, if you can't take the time to properly prepare for your role, why should the meeting participants trust you?

Depending on the size of the room and the audience, make sure that there are enough monitors throughout the room so that the entire group can see. Usually a minimum of a 25-inch monitor strategically placed will do the trick. The session will come to a halt if participants are craning their necks to see a small screen at the front of the room, or if no one can hear the media. Review the room configuration suggestions in step 2 for more tips on ensuring the space is set up so everyone can see.

Plan to show only short segments of the video—no more than 10 to 15 minutes each—before stopping and discussing the content. Working professionals value their time. Having them attend a meeting and then sit through a 30-minute video, unless the video is the only medium to convey the message, shows a lack of respect for everyone's hectic schedules.

As is true for any visual aid, proper use needs to always be top of mind. Do not use video when:

- **Your time is limited**—Videos often stimulate discussion. The content will not be very valuable if you do not have time to discuss it.
- **If you're unsure of the appropriateness of the video**—Always err on the side of caution when selecting content for your meeting. As with humor, avoid any bad language or impolite subject matter.

## Handouts

Handouts usually consist of either additional information related to the facilitation session or the agenda, worksheets, and so on. Handouts are important for a number of reasons:

- They free participants to listen and actively discuss information rather than frantically take notes.
- They enable you to provide additional information to participants that you might not be able to fully cover due to time constraints.
- They enable participants to personalize the materials by highlighting important information and jotting down ideas to share with the group.

As with any other visual aid, handouts need to look professional. Be careful not to use too many different font styles and proof the pages to ensure that there are no misspellings. Staple or paperclip the handouts to make them easier to distribute and to ensure that participants receive all the pages.

STEP 5

You now have a solid understanding of the variety of media choices available to enhance your facilitation session. Use Tool 5-2 to make sure you have selected the right technology for your needs.

## TOOL 5-2
## MEDIA AND TECHNOLOGY PLANNING CHECKLIST

Use this checklist to ensure that you have considered all media implications when preparing to facilitate a meeting.

**The media selected:**
- Incorporates the appropriate amount of movement for facilitator and participant activities.
- Maintains an appropriate level of formality or informality.
- Provides an appropriate level of intellectual interactivity.
- Includes an appropriate level of activity for the time of day.
- Involves an appropriate amount of light in the room for the time of day.
- Is the correct medium for the variability and evolution of the session agenda and facilitation processes.
- Is portable and can be modified on the fly, if needed.

**You've prepared for facilitating using media by:**
- incorporating a variety of media into the session
- assessing the physical environment and matching the best media to the environment
- planning for backup media, just in case
- obtaining permission for material obtained (for example, copyright approvals, if necessary).

*Used with permission from McCain (2015).*

## The Next Step

You know what you need to accomplish, who you're working with, and how you plan to structure the meeting, and now you've selected the best media to help you in that purpose. With the meeting underway, the next step in successful facilitation includes using strategies to keep things on track. Facilitators use a variety of techniques to help participants maintain focus, stay on topic, and move forward toward the meeting's goals in a productive way. The next step will provide you with a toolkit of strategies to keep the meeting on track and moving forward.

# Step 6

# Keep the Meeting Moving and Accomplish Objectives

## Overview

- Keep the facilitation session on track.
- Communicate effectively.
- Accomplish meeting objectives.

Long before the meeting started, you and the person who called the meeting outlined clear, measurable, time-bound outcomes. At the beginning of the meeting you reviewed these outcomes with the participants and hopefully came to an agreement that they were achievable. But even well-planned meetings can go astray and, before you know it, the time is up. As a facilitator, it's your job to make sure discussions and activities stick tightly to the time constraints and drive toward desired outcomes.

It's not just about watching the clock, however; keeping a meeting on track is more art than science. For example, perhaps a group that has had trouble getting along is finally having a friendly discussion, although it's way off topic. Or, a brainstorming session revealed a solution to an unrelated problem—important to this group, but irrelevant to the meeting objectives. Use the following tips to understand when to let the group continue down their path, when to reel them in, and how to communicate effectively to accomplish the objectives. Tool 6-1 presents an overview of some facilitation tips that will be discussed in more detail.

## TOOL 6-1
## FACILITATION TIPS

| Tip | Explanation |
|-----|-------------|
| Ask questions to gain participation | Ask open-ended questions that invite response, especially "what" and "how" questions. Close-ended questions (such as "yes or no" questions) stifle participation. Use close-ended questions only when you want to end discussion and move on. |
| Use transitions | Participants need to know when one topic has closed and another has begun. Transitions don't have to be fancy. A statement as simple as "Now that we have discussed X, let's move on to Y" works well. |
| Control discussions | Regardless of the participation level, help the group work effectively and guide them during discussions to achieve objectives. That means that you need to remind the group of time. If a discussion is taking longer than planned, pose options—for example, the group can continue with the discussion and remove something else from the agenda or table the current discussion until another time. Interrupt when needed to keep the discussion on track. |
| Remain neutral | If the group gets into a debate, clarify and summarize both sides and then move on. Don't express your own opinion (unless the debate concerns a factual matter) because participants with an opposing view may feel put down or that you are not being fair on a certain topic. |
| Don't wing it | Winging it carries some very big risks. You might go on time-consuming tangents, you might lead yourself into a discussion that is not appropriate, or you might steal your own thunder for a later subject. |
| Affirm | Find something to reinforce and affirm in every comment. You can always affirm a person's effort at participation. When you treat people with respect, they will feel comfortable participating. |

| Tip | Explanation |
|---|---|
| Watch and respond to body language | When you see furrowed brows and puzzled looks, ask the group if they understand. For example, you may say, "Some of you look a little puzzled. Is something not making sense?" |
| Don't be afraid of silence | Sometimes people are simply thinking and need a little time. When you ask a question, mentally count to 10 (slowly!) before rephrasing or redirecting the question. |
| Debrief thoroughly | Plan key questions that you will ask at the end of an activity or session to be sure that the participants are actively engaged—and as much as possible, come to consensus on topics or ideas. Do not ad-lib a debriefing session! |

*Used with permission from McCain (2015).*

## Tips to Keep the Facilitation Session on Track

Effective meetings rely heavily on excellent use of facilitation techniques both to keep the session on track and to complete each activity. To keep the session and participants on task consider these tips, which are categorized by the factors that affect a meeting's progress.

### Schedule

- **Stick to the agenda**—The agenda is your road map to accomplishing the defined objectives. Follow it. Deviate only if you confirm with the group that a discussion is taking longer than planned. If the group decides to continue discussing the subject, adjust the timetable as needed; if they decide to table the topic, stick to the agenda timing.

- **Keep individuals on track**—Gently interrupt if any participant gets off the subject for more than a few seconds. Make sure no participant uses the facilitation session as a platform to vent personal frustrations about unrelated matters.

**POINTER**

The most expensive element of any facilitated meeting is the time people spend away from their regular job duties. Keep the group focused on its objectives and moving to a successful outcome to ensure that time isn't wasted.

- **Provide necessary breaks**—Don't wait for signs of restlessness by participants; call a short break once a meeting runs longer than 90 minutes.
- **Put it in a parking lot**—Discussions can raise a lot of questions and ideas that won't contribute to the purpose of the meeting but are nonetheless valuable. Use a parking lot to record such ideas on a flipchart or whiteboard (learn more about the parking lot in step 3). That way you will have a record of those ideas to follow up on at another time. Individuals can also get unrelated concerns heard, let go of any baggage they may be carrying, and return to focusing on the topic at hand.
- **Review periodically**—At appropriate points in the meeting, summarize and review what has been accomplished so far and clarify what remains to be done. This will help the group to stay on track and achieve the meeting objectives.

## Participation

- **Maintain a productive climate**—Model the behavior that you expect participants to follow. Listen closely. Speak frankly. Encourage feedback and accept criticism professionally. Keep an open mind. Evaluate ideas, not people. Positively reinforce creative thinking. Do not dominate the meeting.
- **Encourage and structure participation**—Call on group members for input and ensure that only one person speaks at a time.
- **Ask good questions**—Use open-ended questions to encourage participation and discussion. Avoid leading, personal, trick, or unanswerable questions.
- **Provide constructive feedback**—Make sure feedback is useful and includes positive or neutral statements.
- **Observe participants**—Besides listening to participants, observe their behavior. Watch for signs of boredom, frustration, and other productivity reducers; then deal promptly with the problem. Energize the group with an activity or challenging questions; address causes of frustration, and so forth.

- **Maintain professionalism and enthusiasm**—Show interest in activities and display patience with participants throughout. Set an upbeat, productive example for participants whose energy may wane.

## Interpersonal

- **Give or get clarification of vague statements**—Persist until the intended meaning is clear. Participants will otherwise interpret according to their individual experiences, sparking later disagreements and time-wasting backtracking to figure out what was meant. (Remember the "wilderness" example from step 4.)
- **Discourage generalizations**—If participants generalize or use stereotypes, ask them to evaluate the accuracy of their statements. Query these individuals for specific examples to help clarify responses.
- **Protect minority opinions**—Ensure that the least popular opinions get a full hearing and respect.
- **Reduce tensions**—Gently interrupt if conflicts between participants get out of hand and threaten to destroy meeting effectiveness. Do not deny or bury conflict, but try to help participants sort out their differences professionally.
- **Reframe comments**—Rephrasing any judgmental or accusatory comments and posing them back to the group helps to neutralize potentially charged comments and keeps the focus on the issues. This technique helps group members to hear each other in impartial language so that they can continue to move forward with discussions and accomplish objectives.

**POINTER**

Use reframing to encourage participants to understand one another's point of view and to minimize any personal conflicts among group members.

## Virtual

- **For virtual meetings**—Discourage multitasking by keeping the participants engaged. Call on people by name in a conversational way, even if they haven't "raised their hand," to keep them on their toes. Also use polling or survey tools to ask questions and show the results immediately to keep the group interested.

## Choose the Right Facilitation Techniques to Accomplish Session Objectives

Once the facilitation session has opened, the next step is to guide the group toward the desired outcomes. For example, an outcome might be for the group to create a list of 10 suggestions to assess the current morale of a particular department. This may be accomplished via questioning techniques to gauge participants' current knowledge of the situation and charts and graphs to display survey data. In addition to the specific techniques explored later in this step, use the following general tips throughout the session:

- **Listen**—If you expect the group members to actively participate, then you need to listen to what they are saying. After posing a question, pause and give them time to think and formulate their responses. When someone begins to respond, avoid assuming that you know what they are going to say. Nothing dampens a group's discussions faster than a facilitator who interrupts or jumps to hasty conclusions about a particular point—which may be incorrect. Pose a question, give the audience time to think, and then truly listen to participant input. Let the group drive the discussions—your role is to guide them to the stated outcomes.
- **Accept different opinions and views**—If you are asking for ideas, comments, and thoughts on a topic, be prepared for views that differ from yours. If answers to questions aren't quite on target, then redirect the question and open it up to others by asking, "What do the rest of you think?"
- **Know when to keep silent**—Silence is a surprisingly effective facilitation technique, and one that novice facilitators often struggle with. Pausing enables the group to process what you are saying and to form their own thoughts and opinions.

The next sections delve into additional facilitation techniques to enable healthy discussions. These include questioning techniques, transitions, guided discussion, storytelling, humor, quotations, metaphors, analogies, and the use of tables and graphs.

## Questioning Techniques

Questioning is probably the most common way to encourage participation from a group—and is a skill that serves business professionals both inside and outside of a meeting room. There are several types of questions, including open ended, close ended, hypothetical, and rhetorical. The ability to ask strong questions requires skill, practice, and planning. As a facilitator, remember that your goal is to help participants do the work. Be careful not to ask leading questions—questions that suggest an answer—as that would reflect your thoughts rather than the group's. For example, rather than ask, "Would using sales quota as a metric improve performance?" ask, "Which metrics might improve performance?"

### Open-Ended Questions

Open-ended questions do not have yes or no answers. They usually require participants to respond by expressing their thoughts, ideas, feelings, and opinions. For example:

- "Based on what we've discussed so far, how do you think this new process will affect your job?"
- "What do you think you need to be successful with this new process change?"
- "How do you think you can begin to implement this process change now?"

Asking an open-ended question is an excellent way of getting the participants involved in the meeting, increasing the energy level of the session, and generating group synergy. Open-ended questions often start with:

- "Tell me about . . . "
- "Why . . . ?"
- "What do you think about . . . ?"
- "How . . . ?"

Usually questions that start this way help the participants to expound on their answers, revealing information that can be helpful in discussion.

## Close-Ended Questions

Close-ended questions are preferable to open-ended ones in certain situations. Closed-ended questions are excellent for getting at specific facts and information.

For example, what if group participants were expected to read information about a new process change prior to attending the presentation? You could ask a closed-ended question requiring a yes or no response to gauge how many read the information, such as: "How many of you had a chance to read the information that I sent last week about the new process change?" You aren't interested at this point in whether they agree with or are excited about the change, only the percentage of the group that has some baseline understanding of the topic to be discussed. Closed questions have clearly defined, often factual answers, and usually begin with:

- "Who . . . ?"
- "Where . . . ?"
- "When . . . ?"
- "Did you . . . ?"

## Hypothetical Questions

Hypothetical questions are great to get people thinking freely in situations in which many answers may be valid. They often start with "What if . . . ?"

For example, "What if we could implement a new process that would reduce the amount of time you spend on this task by 50 percent every day?"

Hypothetical questions are excellent discussion starters because they allow the participants to internalize a situation; think through any issues, problems, or solutions; and then actively discuss the impact and their ideas. One warning—because hypothetical questions are so effective at getting the audience to open up and join in the discussion, as a facilitator you may need to rein things in a bit to meet the agenda time constraints.

### Rhetorical Questions

Rhetorical questions—while really not questions at all—get the group thinking when you don't really expect them to answer the question aloud. These types of questions are used to create excitement or interest in the topics and discussions to come.

For example, "We've all heard about the new process change, and I know that change is sometimes difficult. But have I told you that this new process has been proven to reduce workflow downtime by 50 percent?"

The success of rhetorical questions, just like the other facilitation techniques discussed in this section, is directly related to how you ask the question as much as what you ask. When using this technique, vary the pace of your speech to emphasize key words and then end with silence. Allow the participants time to process what you have said because rhetorical questions are a great way to prime a group to discuss a topic.

### Guided Discussion Questions

Guided discussions are a structured exercise consisting of a series of planned questions designed to get participants to wrestle with topics and issues at a deeper level. As they answer the questions, the facilitator summarizes their content, may also play devil's advocate to drive for deeper content or application, and guides the discussion to the next question.

## Transitions

Transitions help you smoothly move from one part of the agenda to another, or from one specific point to another. They are segues to the different segments of the meeting and are important in making the facilitation session cohesive and understandable. For example, once the group appears to have reached consensus on a topic, check for agreement from the group: "So are we all in agreement? Jack, did we address your concerns? Is everyone okay with the definitions and tasks we outlined for these job roles?"

## Storytelling

Stories are memorable, people like to hear them, and they are a useful technique to capture an audience's attention and illustrate key points. We all know presenters, facilitators, and leaders who seem to have an innate ability to tell stories. They are able to pull out an appropriate tale, with a poignant message, just right for the situation or audience at hand. Good storytelling is a learned skill that comes with practice. You can start a story to get discussions going and leave the rest of the story for later. Or, you can begin the story and then ask the group, "What do you think happened next?"

When thinking through story development, remember that a good story has a beginning and an end. Consider the best point in time to begin your story, and develop an engaging start to draw in participants. Think about the pinnacle moments in the story and how you can leverage them for maximum impact. And of course, your story should have a natural and clear ending. Practice telling the story a few times prior to the facilitation session.

Perhaps the most important characteristic of an effective storyteller is the ability to remain authentic—that is, staying true to your own stories and maintaining the integrity of stories you select to retell. This means sharing truthful and relevant facts and details. Authenticity also shows on your face. When you are truly engaged in the story, the group can tell by your facial expressions and body language. By sharing the emotion you feel in the telling of the story, you help the audience resonate with you and your key point.

Winging it with examples and stories doesn't work. You can get off schedule in a big way. If you select a story to tell on the spot, you might be stealing your thunder for an important point later. You might get to the end only to discover that the main point isn't really relevant to the content at hand. Some presenters even get to the end of a spur-of-the-moment story and realize that not only does it not make a point, but the punch line is also offensive. Think through your examples and stories before you begin.

## Humor

Humor and laughter help maintain and enhance participant interest in a meeting. Camaraderie begins to develop when the facilitator and participants share a pun, story, or other common experience. Humor fosters a team atmosphere and promotes a positive experience.

Here are some tips for using humor, jokes, and funny stories during facilitation sessions:

- Keep it relevant. Jokes that tie to the subject matter can add some comic relief or segue into new topics. Telling a funny story that doesn't have anything to do with the meeting can be distracting and a misuse of valuable time.
- Avoid humor that might offend or alienate participants. If you wouldn't tell your modest aunt the story or joke, steer clear. And, even if your audience appears comfortable with curse words, it's never appropriate for the facilitator to swear. Remember that this is a professional event, even if the group appears casual.
- Laugh at yourself, particularly when a story or pun flops. This puts the participants at ease and indicates that you are comfortable with the group and self-confident about your facilitation skills.

## Quotations

Quotations from others that are strategically planned in the beginning, middle, or end of your facilitation session often have the effect of stimulating people's thinking. Before you use a quote, however, be sure of its authenticity—especially if you found it online—and its relevance to the subject matter. When you use a quote, always give attribution to the appropriate source.

## Metaphors and Analogies

Metaphors are thought-provoking forms of speech that open people's minds to think differently about a subject or issue. Metaphors compare two things by describing one as another. For example, "My brother is the black sheep in the family." The man is not literally a sheep; the metaphor means he's unlike the rest of the members of his family.

One presenter at a career development seminar used the New York City Marathon as a metaphor for the effort involved in searching for a new job. He painted a picture in the minds of his audience of the daunting task of running the marathon. He then explained that conducting a job search was similar because those who are successful in completing the journey in the shortest time are always the ones who spent the most time preparing themselves.

An analogy is another form of comparison, typically used to clarify a concept. Analogies, like metaphors, help paint a picture in people's minds so they can "see" concepts more clearly. One facilitator, introducing a new financial reporting system, used this analogy: "My understanding is that trying to reconcile the old monthly financial reports was like putting together a jigsaw puzzle only to find some of the pieces missing." Nodding their heads in agreement, the participants became eager, wanting to learn more about this new, less frustrating system and the project. Analogies differ from metaphors because the comparison is spelled out, rather than implicit; analogies generally use the words "like" or "as" to make it clear that the speaker is comparing two things.

## Tables and Graphs

To help participants understand data, consider using a table or graph to organize the information. For example, you might use a graph to illustrate data in support of a problem and then ask the group to come up with solutions. Or, the group might have taken a survey before the meeting, and you use a chart to share the results, broken into different categories.

Be prepared to clarify (or have an expert available who can clarify) the statistical meaning of the data and the implications, and provide sources if necessary. Be sure to proofread the data and ensure the accuracy of the numbers and calculations.

Don't make graphs too complicated; readability and the ability to understand the information are the keys to making the graph effective. As a general guideline, the audience should be able to read and understand the graph in fewer than 30 seconds. Be careful not to exaggerate the data points by changing the scale (for example, 0–100 or 1–50) or gridlines in the background to make something look more significant than it really is. Tick marks often clutter a graph, so use them sparingly and only if they add clarity for the audience. Gridlines or other graph elements that do not add clarity should be omitted.

Graphs are an effective way to present data, show trends, and demonstrate relationships. However, some graphs are more effective at accomplishing these goals than others. In general:

- **Bar graphs**—Show relationships between two or more variables at one time or at several points in time. Improve the readability of a bar chart by making the bars wider than the spaces between them.
- **Line graphs**—Show a progression of changes over time. Be sure to label axes, data lines, and data points clearly.
- **Pie charts**—Show the relationships between the parts of a unit at a given moment. Include only essential information in pie charts and avoid having more than six wedges of the pie. Smaller pie slices can always be lumped into an "other" category.

## Read the Room and Communicate Effectively

Questions, stories, humor, and charts can provide structure and direction to a meeting, but a facilitator must also be adept at reading the room and acting responsively to participant behavior throughout each activity. Everything that goes on in a facilitation session involves both verbal and nonverbal communication. The group shares ideas, listens, questions, and makes decisions. But someone may feel alienated based on the nonverbal communication of other group members. For example, if one chatty group member begins to speak and other participants instantly roll their eyes, this behavior sends a message loud and clear not only to the speaker but to other group members as well. Experienced facilitators communicate effectively with groups using both verbal and nonverbal techniques and encourage this same behavior from the group participants.

## POINTER

Successful facilitators know how to actively engage a group. They say the right things in the right ways to invite input and keep it coming! The following are simple feedback phrases that work to encourage future participation. Next are the phrases that facilitators should avoid–these items quickly close the doors on communication!

**Say:**
- I'm glad you brought that up. That's an interesting thought.
- Let's build on that.
- You're on the right track. What else?
- Good idea. Who else has a suggestion?

**Avoid:**
- Too risky. Let someone else try that first.
- That won't work.
- We tried that once and it didn't work.
- It will cost too much.
- It will take too much time.
- It's not practical.
- We never do things like that.

## Verbal Communication Skills

Verbal communication can immediately engage or irritate a group. Voice inflection enables facilitators to capture a group's attention and hold its interest. In any meeting, how you say something is just as important as what you are saying. To improve your verbal communication, sharpen these skills:

- **Projection**—The group has to be able to hear you and other participants in every part of the room. Depending on the acoustics in the meeting room, be prepared to ratchet up your voice projection, and avoid inadvertently dropping the volume after the first few sentences of the meeting opening.

As a best practice, repeat some comments or questions from meeting participants to ensure that all group members can hear and follow the dialog.

- **Pitch**—The dreaded monotone voice has lulled many a participant to sleep. Avoid droning on, never modulating the pitch of your voice up or down. Having a monotone delivery is usually the result of paying more attention to saying the exact words listed on the facilitator outline rather than listening to how you are saying the words. Let the group hear a change in your pitch when you are excited about an upcoming point, the discussion, or an activity. Modulate the pitch of your voice to accentuate more serious information. The group will take its cues not only from what you say, but—sometimes even more important—how you say it.

- **Pronunciation**—If the group can't understand what you are saying, it's as if you didn't say it at all. Successful facilitators demonstrate exceptional diction—the art of speaking precisely so that each word is clearly heard and understood to its fullest. Be sure to enunciate each word clearly when facilitating, using questioning techniques or rephrasing. In certain parts of the country, slight dialects may be difficult to understand until listeners' ears get attuned to the sound and how specific words are pronounced. Keep this in mind if you have an accent or when facilitating meetings in certain areas of the country or abroad.

- **Pace**—Good facilitators adjust their rate of speaking to accentuate a feeling or mood. Although the average rate of speech is about 140 words per minute, to show enthusiasm or energy for a particular point try increasing the number of words accordingly. To emphasize an important point, try slowing down the rate to as few as 100 words per minute. This isn't science, so you don't have to get out a stopwatch and count. Rather, understand that you can create a mood and atmosphere for your meeting just by how you use your voice.

STEP 6

- **Pauses and fillers**—Pauses can add emphasis in just the right parts of any facilitated meeting. For example, a carefully placed pause can help to focus attention on a topic before a group activity or before transitioning to a new topic. Pauses after you pose an idea or question also provide time for the group to think about what you're saying. By pausing and remaining silent, you encourage the group to share their thoughts or provide feedback.

Meanwhile, fillers are those words that creep into your speech to fill silence while you are thinking or transitioning to a new thought—they include *uh, um, er, ah, OK, right,* and *you know.* Filler words are one of the fastest ways to annoy a group and even turn their focus to jotting down tick marks every time you use one. Don't be afraid to pause and leave silence between your sentences and thoughts. Skilled, confident facilitators are comfortable with silence and use it effectively to get the group to react to what was said and share opinions or ideas.

## Nonverbal Communication Skills

Body language—meaning how you look and move—can enhance or undermine your facilitation skills. Based on different studies, it is usually accepted that between seven and 10 percent of the effectiveness of a meeting comes from the words the facilitator uses. Because the remaining 90 percent of meeting effectiveness is attributed to nonverbal communication, facilitators need to be cognizant of their body language (and that of the group as well) and use gestures, eye contact, and facial expressions to enhance communication and sharing of ideas. When facilitating virtual sessions, if at all possible, select a meeting software with a videoconferencing option so your group doesn't miss out on these important nonverbal communication cues.

Many new facilitators struggle with exactly what they should be doing with their hands and bodies when guiding a group. For example, should they lean on or grip the table for security? Rock or sway? Stand poker straight with hands at their sides? Cross their arms in front of their chests? The answer is—none of these! Keep in mind that a facilitation session is about the participants. As such, the facilitator needs to disappear into the background and let the group run with ideas and discussions. Because facilitators aren't invisible, they need to use body language and gestures effectively to help communication—to emphasize, show agreement, and maintain group interest. In general, use movement when you want to convey enthusiasm and energy about a particular point or result of an activity during the meeting, ultimately using your body language to emphasize the point of the meeting and engage participants, not to draw attention to yourself. Seasoned facilitators walk to different parts of the room while making eye contact with the group members, especially if they are working in subgroups or on assigned activities. Movement can be used to engage all the group members, especially if you approach different areas of the room. This technique keeps everyone focused as you help to guide the group through a process for them to achieve the session objectives.

Gestures refer to hand and body movements that are part of communication. When you watch a play, the actors use gestures to convey emotions, add emphasis to particular points, paint a mental picture, and so on. Consider these points regarding body language and gestures when facilitating a meeting:

- **Assume a good stance**—Taking a natural stance is important when facilitating a session. You want to project a comfortable, confident image, without appearing too casual. As a general rule, stand with legs about 18 inches apart or so (depending on your size), and equally distribute your weight on each foot, with your arms in a comfortable position at your sides or lightly resting on the table if you are seated.

- **Pay attention to and eliminate unconscious body language**—Some gestures and movements can distract the group. Such distractions include fidgeting, pacing, clicking a pen cap, and jingling keys or coins in pockets.

## POINTER

Use effective gestures to help convey information and engage the participants' interest. This helps to show your enthusiasm about the meeting and interest in the group and adds energy to the group. Your interest and enthusiasm are often contagious!

- **Use gestures for emphasis**—For example, if you say, "There are three steps in the new workflow process," hold up three fingers sequentially as you articulate each point.
- **Observe the audience's body language**—Facial expressions, down-turned eyes, looks of concern, fidgeting, or slouching are all signs of boredom, lack of interest, or lack of understanding.
- **Use positive facial expressions**—Include smiles, expressive eyes, looks of concern, empathy, and encouragement. Look at your face in the mirror. How do you communicate feelings and emotions? How do you use your eyes, eyebrows, and mouth to express yourself?
- **Make eye contact**—Show the group that you are engaging with them. How much eye contact is appropriate? As a general rule, spend five or six seconds of eye contact at least once with each member of the group, making sure that you look at everyone when facilitating. Eye contact is also an opportunity for a facilitator to get a feel for how the group is reacting to the meeting, discussions, and other participants.
- **Never sit behind a desk or stand behind a podium for the entire session**—This establishes a barrier between you and the group. Put more life into the meeting by moving freely about the room. Facilitators who trap themselves behind the podium and venture out occasionally to write on a flipchart appear less than enthusiastic and confident.
- **Walk toward participants as they respond to your questions**—This encourages them to continue. As a participant responds, nod your head slowly to show you hear what they are saying. If you need to think through what has been asked or to clarify the question, consider paraphrasing the question back or say, "So if I understand your question, you are asking . . . "

Above all, demonstrate interest in the topic and the opportunity to facilitate. Your enthusiasm is contagious and often increases attention and optimism from the group.

# Accomplish Meeting Objectives

Being on track in a meeting means that the group is progressing with the agenda and is moving toward accomplishing the agreed-upon objectives. If the meeting has been well planned and the meeting outcomes were well defined, reaching the end of the agenda should also mean the group has accomplished its objectives, whether finalizing a decision or brainstorming new ideas.

That doesn't mean that the group needs to strictly follow the agenda minute by minute, however. As a facilitator, you need to allow the group enough latitude for creative discussions, brainstorming, activities, and healthy disagreements as long as they are helping to achieve the stated outcomes. When trying to determine whether to let a discussion continue, or if it's time to get the group back on track, consider these guidelines:

- Review the agenda and determine if the time constraints allow for more discussion or if you need to gently interrupt.
- Review the ground rules regarding discussions that aren't relevant to the agenda and achieving the session objectives. If the discussion is relevant, but is throwing the agenda timing off, ask the group if they want to continue with the discussion (at the sacrifice of something else), or if the discussion should be put in the parking lot until another time to follow the agenda's timing.
- Assess why the group has gone off track. Confirm that the group members are clear about the session objectives. For example, are participants focused on their own needs over the needs of the group (for example, airing their personal frustrations rather than focusing on the topic at hand)?
- Point out the remaining agenda items, remind the group what needs to be accomplished, and help them to understand the time requirements.
- If one person is getting sidetracked, ask them to explain how their comments link to the topic or objectives to try to get the conversation back on track.

STEP 6

- Offer your unbiased observations—for example, by saying "I'm sensing that the group is having a bit of heartburn about the new pension plan." Try to uncover the core issue and get the group back on track with the topics and the agenda—or get the group to agree on what items should be removed from the agenda if more time is to be spent on the current topic.
- Post the meeting objectives. As the group makes a decision or reaches an important milestone, write it down on the same flipchart or whiteboard. Keep track of how many more steps or decisions need to be made. If a discussion continues too long or the group veers from the agenda too far, remind the group how much more work there is to do.
- Recap decisions and action items. As decisions are made, review the group's progress and any action items that need to be accomplished after the meeting. To ensure accountability, write down the due date and person responsible next to each action item.
- Drive toward closure, action, and next steps. Every activity and discussion should get the group one step closer to its objectives. Keep the group tightly focused and help to build consensus so decisions can be made.

## The Next Step

As the group progresses toward its goals conflict is inevitable, even among the healthiest teams. The next step is to create an environment that encourages constructive dialogue and diminishes disruption.

# Step 7

# Leverage Strategies to Develop Teams and Deal With Conflict

## Overview

- Follow the stages of team development.
- Recognize behaviors that enhance or hinder effectiveness.
- Identify and manage difficult participants.

STEP 7

Effective groups don't just happen. Any time a work group is formed, individuals bring their own preconceived thoughts and beliefs to the table. Depending on the organization, there may be additional group dynamics at work, such as norms and organizational culture. The size of the group, whether it is formal or informal, and the type of leadership also affect the group.

Facilitators need to know enough about the group to maximize group participation, productivity, and satisfaction; they also need to have a solid understanding of people, groups, facilitating styles, and the stages of team development.

## Stages of Team Development

Teams often generate a tremendous amount of positive energy when they are first formed. Members are excited, motivated, and ready to roll up their sleeves and tackle tasks immediately. As individuals join together, the group takes on a new life of its own. Groups can even go through stages of development comparable to the stages of individual growth: infancy, childhood, adolescence, adulthood, and old age. Each stage has its own characteristics and requirements, and each builds on the preceding phases.

Although the stages of development are sequentially predictable, each group is unique in how it progresses and regresses through these stages. Some phases can be more painful than others; sometimes groups get stuck in a particular stage and cannot advance.

Although numerous classifications of group development stages exist, Bruce Tuckman and Mary Jane Jensen (1997) have identified five stages that capture strategies for dealing with group conflict:

1. forming
2. storming
3. norming
4. performing
5. adjourning.

## Forming

During this stage, group members tend to be extremely polite. They seek guidance and may be reluctant to participate. Serious topics and expression of personal feelings are avoided. At this stage, the group needs to get acquainted, share personal information, and begin to develop relationships (the acquainters discussed in step 3 are good tools for this stage). Members should explore their similarities and orient themselves toward the task they've been assigned. To grow to the next stage, group members must be willing to confront threatening topics and risk the possibility of conflict.

Facilitators can support forming by:

- planning introductions, sharing members' skills, background, and interests
- reviewing the agenda and stating the desired outcomes
- using warm-up activities

- soliciting and listening to expectations from the participants
- establishing ground rules
- agreeing on decision-making methods.

## Storming

As groups move from the forming stage, they may ask questions such as:

- Who is responsible for what?
- What are the rules?
- What are the "hidden agendas?"
- Are there "invisible committees?"

During this stage, some of the initial excitement from the beginning of the meeting has worn off and the reality of the tasks at hand sets in. Personalities begin to emerge; boundaries are tested, power struggles or conflicts develop, and cliques form. Some members may remain silent, whereas others attempt to dominate. As a facilitator, you are not spared from the conflict of this stage. Participants may question or test your authority. Groups often fail at this stage because they encounter conflict they cannot resolve. Participants may feel frustration or anger with the team's progress and may begin to wonder if the group can achieve its goals.

Conflict at this stage is normal; in fact, if a group is so polite that they try to avoid any conflict (and therefore this stage of group development), they are less likely to accomplish their task. Avoidance usually results in more significant conflict later in the meeting or after it ends, which is difficult to resolve.

To grow from this stage to the next, group members must be willing to give up personal preferences in favor of the requirements of the total group. The group members need to listen, avoid defensive attitudes, confront others in a positive way, and be willing to influence and be influenced. Keep in mind that not every conflict is harmful—conflict can be healthy!

Establish ground rules. Ground rules detail the standards of behavior that the group expects of each participant. The group should develop the ground rules and can add to them as needed. The facilitator's role is to enforce the ground rules, but often the group self-polices.

STEP 7

At this point in the process, facilitators can help guide the group by addressing the storming issues of the group, modeling appropriate behavior, and promoting good conflict-resolution processes, including:

- separating problems from the individuals
- not taking storming issues personally
- enforcing ground rules
- acting as the process expert.

## Norming

When groups move from storming to norming, they begin merging into a cohesive team with more cooperation and understanding. The group has negotiated roles, successfully manages differences of opinion, develops both written and unwritten rules, recognizes the need for interdependence, and masters decision-making mechanics. The group is now ready to tackle the task and feels more confident about its ability to achieve its goals. Storming sometimes overlaps with norming; if new tasks are introduced, requiring participants to demonstrate new strengths and weaknesses, conflicts may emerge again. Hopefully, each time this happens the group will be able to resolve with increasing ease and efficiency, as participants get to know each other and understand how to work together.

Unfortunately, many groups do not make it to this stage. If a group has not established positive relationships during its early stages, or if conflict remains unresolved, these factors will impede the group's ability to make effective decisions.

At this point in the group development process, the facilitator should:

- Observe emerging norms.
- Encourage the expression of differences positively.
- Encourage group cohesiveness.
- Facilitate negotiation.

**POINTER**

Establishing trust is critical to reducing conflict in groups; this is especially true with virtual meetings. Be sure to establish and follow ground rules to help foster a respectful environment.

## Performing

The move from the norming to performing is characterized by a high level of trust. Members are recognized for, and encouraged to use, their unique talents; they also understand one another's strengths and weaknesses and how each contributes to the group. The team is typically able to resolve or even prevent conflicts, and members may also feel positive about the group's progress. Once the group has reached this stage, it's possible for much of the work to be accomplished and a consensus reached.

Paradoxically, when a group is highly cohesive and long lived, it is also susceptive to "group think." Group think occurs when individual members suppress their objections and criticisms so that the group can reach agreement with minimal conflict. As a result, the group will make riskier, less thoughtful decisions.

Facilitators should support the group by:

- guiding the group through effective processes to accomplish the desired outcomes
- avoiding the temptation to mediate unless the group is truly stuck and floundering.

STEP 7

## Adjourning

During this last stage, the group prepares to wrap up. In a facilitated session, groups typically adjourn at the scheduled time or once the work is complete. Groups that meet regularly over a long period of time may disband because their work is complete, because the company's needs have changed, or because group members no longer feel challenged by the task. As the team adjourns, members may feel satisfied with the work accomplished; although as this stage approaches, some team members may lose interest, thinking the bulk of the work has already been done.

To aid groups through these developmental stages, facilitators can:

- Establish a climate that encourages and recognizes participation.
- Make sure tasks are completed.
- Listen intently, synthesize, and restate various viewpoints.
- "Take the group's pulse" to understand and recognize where members are and where they need to be.
- Describe what is going on and what is unspoken.
- Find areas of agreement and common threads.
- Design and apply a variety of techniques and processes to encourage creativity and productivity.
- Be flexible.

Research suggests that virtual teams do not develop exactly as in-person teams. According to Russell Haines (2014), the virtual context—including the limitations of using phones or computers to communicate—increases pressure to conform. Trust develops as the team successfully makes progress toward its goal, and, as the team continues to achieve, the trust bonds increase. To help virtual teams develop healthy dynamics, Haines suggests facilitators set clear, specific goals; help participants speak freely to each other; and, if groups will work together again in the future, encourage participants to value the team development.

## Recognize Behaviors That Enhance or Hinder Group Effectiveness

How do facilitators determine exactly whether participants are either increasing or decreasing the group's effectiveness throughout the stages of team development? Successful facilitators follow these phases:

- Phase 1: Observe Behaviors
- Phase 2: Track Frequency of Behaviors
- Phase 3: Determine Whether It Is Appropriate to Mediate
- Phase 4: Describe the Behavior and Provide Feedback.

## Phase 1: Observe Behaviors

The ground rules established at the start of the facilitation session outline one set of agreed-upon behaviors. Participants displaying behavior counter to those ground rules are most likely being ineffective or disruptive. Tool 7-1 summarizes behaviors common in a typical group in three broad categories:

- **Task functions**—Facilitate the group in selecting, defining, and solving a common problem.
- **Maintenance functions**—Alter or maintain the way in which group members interact.
- **Individual functions**—May help or hinder the group's progress.

## TOOL 7-1

### SUMMARY OF TASK, MAINTENANCE, AND INDIVIDUAL BEHAVIORS

| Functions | Behavior | Definition |
|---|---|---|
| Task Activity | Initiating | Proposing tasks or goals, defining the problem, suggesting a procedure or ideas for solving the problem |
| | Information seeking | Requesting facts, seeking relevant data about a problem, asking for suggestions or ideas |
| | Clarifying | Clearing up confusion, indicating alternatives, giving examples |
| | Summarizing | Restating suggestions, synthesizing ideas, offering a decision or direction for the group to accept or reject |
| | Consensus testing | Setting up straw men to see if the group is near conclusion, checking to see how much agreement has been reached |

STEP 7

| Functions | Behavior | Definition |
|---|---|---|
| Maintenance Activity | Encouraging | Being friendly, recognizing others |
| | Expressing group feelings | Sensing moods, feelings, relationships with others, sharing feelings |
| | Harmonizing | Reconciling disagreements, reducing tensions, getting others to explore their differences |
| | Compromising | Admitting error, disciplining oneself to maintain group cohesion |
| | Gatekeeping | Trying to keep communication channels open, suggesting procedures or inducing discussions of group problems |
| | Setting standards | Expressing standards to achieve, applying standards to evaluate the group and its output, evaluating frequently |
| | Coaching and consulting | Working with group members and management outside the building |
| Individual Activity | Blocking | Interfering with group progress by arguing, resisting, disagreeing, or beating a dead horse |
| | Avoiding | Withdrawing from the discussion, daydreaming, doing something else, whispering, leaving the room |
| | Digressing | Going off the subject, filibustering, discussing personal issues |

When observing participants' behaviors, it's important for facilitators to embody a listening mindset. Listening shows an interest in the person who is speaking and a respect for others' experience. When observing your group, listen not only to what is being said but how it is being said.

Facilitators listen actively throughout the meeting, showing a high level of interaction with the speaker, and listen for content, meaning, and feelings. They observe who spoke, exactly what was said, how long the person spoke, at whom individuals look when they speak, who supports whom, any challenges to group leadership, nonverbal communication, side conversations, and lack of participation. Facilitators may ask questions, restate what has been said, summarize positions, or reflect a speaker's feelings. They may also keep track of the different roles group members play.

Occasionally, meeting participants fail to listen to one another or otherwise demonstrate disruptive behavior that requires the facilitator to interrupt a group's discussion or activity because it's no longer effective or appropriate. This means the facilitator must pay careful attention to the group's overall demeanor, as well as the interactions among individual group members.

## Phase 2: Track Frequency of Individual and Group Behaviors

Many facilitators use checklists to track the behaviors—both good and bad—of group members. This allows the facilitator to provide accurate feedback at the end of a meeting. Keeping track of behaviors can make criticism and feedback specific, objective, and, therefore, easier to take. Although charting is a helpful technique, facilitators should get the participants' permission to use it—especially in the early stages when participants may not completely trust each other.

You may want to use Tool 7-2 to track the behaviors of the group you are facilitating. Notice there is one column for group members' names and one column to track the general behavior of the group. During the session, tally how many times an individual or the group engages in a particular behavior. For example, group members may feel that, as a group, they interrupt each other too much. The facilitator may be asked to note that one aspect and report to the team at the end of the meeting. Facilitators can also use the tallies on this worksheet as a confidence builder by tracking various desirable leadership behaviors and reporting back on them. The chart also records any anti-group roles adopted by individuals.

STEP **7**

# Tool 7-2
## Tracking Group and Individual Behaviors

When using this tool, be sure to gain the group's approval and agreement on how the data will be used and discussed. During the session, tally how many times an individual or the group engages in a particular behavior.

| Behaviors | Members | | | | | | Group |
|---|---|---|---|---|---|---|---|
| **Task Activity** | | | | | | | |
| Initiator | | | | | | | |
| Information seeker | | | | | | | |
| Clarifier | | | | | | | |
| Summarizer | | | | | | | |
| Consensus tester | | | | | | | |
| Information giver | | | | | | | |
| **Maintenance Activity** | | | | | | | |
| Encourager | | | | | | | |
| Expresser of group feelings | | | | | | | |
| Harmonizer | | | | | | | |
| Compromiser | | | | | | | |
| Gatekeeper | | | | | | | |
| Standard setter | | | | | | | |
| Coach | | | | | | | |
| Collaborator | | | | | | | |
| **Individual Activity** | | | | | | | |
| Blocker | | | | | | | |
| Avoider | | | | | | | |
| Digressor | | | | | | | |
| Recognition seeker | | | | | | | |
| Dominator | | | | | | | |

## Phase 3: Determine Whether and When to Interrupt

Facilitators often must gently interrupt a group's activity or discussion, for example to redirect the group's focus back to the task at hand or to engage passive participants.

Here are four types of mediations:

- asking the group to examine its dynamics and improve its performance
- encouraging member participation
- encouraging problem solving and decision making
- ensuring compliance with procedures, policies, and ground rules established at the beginning of your meeting, or those set by the organization.

These disruptions are intended to alter the flow of events. They may quicken the development of the group, change the course of the discussion, increase the group's energy, or help the group become more aware of how it is functioning.

Facilitators should not interrupt unless there is reason—for example, when the group wanders off track, when two participants are in conflict, when an individual isn't participating or is angry, or when a participant becomes autocratic. Timing is everything; depending on what is occurring, facilitators may choose to mediate the issue before, during, or after the meeting.

When you do have to interrupt, knowing how to do so carefully and professionally is a required skill of successful facilitators. Consider these guidelines on how to mediate in a group's process:

- **Describe process obstacles**—If nothing is happening, describe the next step and perhaps encourage the contributions of several participants.
- **Encourage participation**—Begin at the start of the meeting and plan activities to maintain that participation throughout the session.

STEP 7

- **Use body language**—Engage people by moving closer to the table or particular participants to either support those who are under fire or to quiet down disruptive members.
- **Discourage personal attacks**—Remind individuals and the group of the ground rules and refocus the discussion on the issue to dissuade personal attacks.
- **Suggest a break**—End a deadlock or simply reenergize the group. Refreshment breaks are common, but others work just as well, such as moving to small breakout groups for a few minutes or taking a five-minute joke break.
- **Summarize**—Go over any problems and solutions that the group generated. Groups may get lost in discussion; summarizing helps the group refocus and keep moving.
- **Have the group manage the process**—Do this as the group matures. Turning over some facilitation duties indicates both trust and respect for the group and its interactions.
- **Debrief the group**—Examine what is happening. Debriefing requires all group members to reflect on the meeting and is usually done at the end of the session. Debriefing may also be useful at natural breaks in the meeting agenda.
- **Search for common threads**—If the group is wandering, stop the meeting and ask for the group to search for what the solution or problem definitions have in common.
- **Present a straw man**—Develop (or suggest that someone develop) a draft problem description or solution during a break. A straw man encourages the group to criticize the plan, attack it, and pull it apart.
- **Act stupid**—This may help participants who are uninvolved or may not understand what is happening or what someone is saying. These participants may not want to volunteer their ignorance. Ask for clarification of issues, problems, terminology, or anything else that may get in the way of consensus later in the process.
- **Get specific**—This will help clear up hard-to-grasp issues, problems, and solutions.

## Phase 4: Describe Behavior and Provide Feedback

When providing feedback regarding disruptive behaviors, you should be descriptive, specific, and mindful of the needs of the group—not individuals. You need to describe what you privately observed in phase one that led you to interrupt. Remember to always use the ground rules that the group agreed to when explaining your observation and interpretation of the behavior. You are using the ground rules to test your assumptions—so this is not a personal attack, just a professional observation to try and help the group function more efficiently. At this point, test whether the group agrees with the observations.

Keep in mind that group members may see things differently. Ask the group whether you have accurately captured the exchange or behaviors. If you misheard or misinterpreted something—and the group calls you on it—then that is a success! The group is policing themselves and sees things differently than you do.

Once you have provided feedback regarding the disruptive behavior and gained group or individual feedback on your observations, the next step is to help the group decide whether to change the group behavior and ground rules. Remember, your role as a facilitator is to guide the group toward successful decision making. An effective facilitator can maximize participation, productivity, and satisfaction and should focus on managing the decision-making process and supporting the group through the various stages of group development.

## Embrace Productive Conflict

Managing disruptive behavior isn't easy. It's a challenge that is unique to each facilitator and each group. The key is to recognize the individual and group thought processes occurring and to select the appropriate response or time to intervene.

The phrase "managing conflict" may be a bit of a misnomer when facilitating meetings. Productive meetings don't necessarily quash conflicts—rather they provide an opportunity to air disagreements and express opinions. The dynamics and synergy result in large leaps forward and generate a plethora of ideas.

STEP 7

To reap the value of conflict, facilitators need to create an environment that allows participants to disagree publicly. In fact, the facilitator's role is to encourage and protect minority opinions. How do facilitators walk a fine line to encourage conflict and opinions while avoiding destructive conflict? Consider these guidelines:

- Look for shared goals and win–win situations.
- Clarify, sort, and value differences.
- Gain commitment to change attitudes and modes of communication when necessary.
- Openly praise group members who are willing to suggest new and different approaches.
- Analyze why conflicts keep occurring—usually participants aren't fighting about what they say they are fighting about.
- Encourage individuals to take the initiative to change personally.
- Model the kind of behavior that shows a comfort level with conflict.

When possible, encourage the use of "I" statements rather than "you" statements to depersonalize conflict. Using "I" statements means turning statements from accusations ("you did . . . ") into statements of fact or personal feeling ("I felt this way when this happened . . . "). Depersonalizing a conflict involves looking at a problem objectively.

## POINTER

Anticipate conflicting views, problems, and challenges. Successful facilitators not only spend time anticipating the differing views and issues that may come up during a facilitation session, but they actively plan which facilitation tools and techniques will be most effective to combat these challenges.

# Identify and Manage Difficult Participants

Individuals in a group often have their own motivations and agendas. How you react to challenging individuals can either enhance or undermine your credibility and either enhance or disrupt the group processes.

Do not take disruptive behavior personally, even if a participant seems to focus on you. Address the specific behavior of the person in order to suggest it's not the person who is disruptive, but what is being done or said. For example, rather than saying "You are interrupting our meeting," say, "I'm having a hard time listening to the group discussion right now. Can the side conversation be postponed until after the meeting?"

**POINTER**

There will be times when your judgment as a facilitator may be called into question—when you believe you must act more firmly or leniently than you would like. Don't let that dissuade you from intervening when the group or individual participants need guidance to get them back on track.

Even the best facilitators experience difficult participants. What do you do if you've referenced the ground rules, addressed the behavior, patiently waited for the disruptor to settle down, but the behavior still continues? First, there are several actions to avoid, including engaging in an argument, insulting the person, or expressing your anger. Second, try to understand whether the conflict is based on a professional disagreement—such as a difference in opinion over a decision made—or a personality struggle between group members. Professional disagreements are healthy and, if the facilitator can continue to engage the group in productive discussions until the conflict is resolved, may result in a better outcome. Personality problems are more difficult to resolve, however. If there's a conflict between two people, you may ask that they find time to take it "offline," meaning outside of the meeting.

A final option is to let the group handle it. The disruptor's own team members will be distracted and most likely annoyed, at least as much as the facilitator, and may ignore that participant, roll their eyes when they speak, or use other negative reinforcement in an effort to quell the disruptor's behavior.

STEP **7**

Tool 7-3 presents many of the disruptive behaviors you might experience, explains why group members may behave that way, and provides suggestions for handling the disruptive behavior.

## TOOL 7-3
### IDENTIFYING AND HANDLING DISRUPTIVE BEHAVIORS

| Behavior | Why It Happens | What to Do |
|---|---|---|
| Heckler | Is probably good natured most of the time but is distracted by job or personal problems | Keep your temper under control.<br><br>Honestly agree with one idea, then move on to something else.<br><br>Toss a misstatement of fact to the group to turn down.<br><br>Talk privately as a last resort to determine what is bothering the person. |
| Rambler | One idea leads to another and takes this person miles away from the original point | When there is a pause for breath, thank them, refocus attention, and move on.<br><br>In a friendly manner, indicate that "We are a little off subject."<br><br>As a last resort, use your agenda timetable. Glance at your watch and say, "Time is limited." |
| Ready Answer | Really wants to help, but makes it difficult by keeping others from participating | Cut this off tactfully by questioning others. Suggest that "we put others to work."<br><br>Ask such people to summarize. It keeps them attentive and capitalizes on their enthusiasm. |
| Conversationalist | Side chatter is usually personal in nature but may be related to topic | Call by name and ask an easy question.<br><br>Call by name, restate the last opinion expressed, and ask their opinion.<br><br>Include them in the discussion. |

STEP 7

| Behavior | Why It Happens | What to Do |
|---|---|---|
| Personality Problems | Two or more individuals clash, dividing the group into factions and endangering the success of the meeting | Maximize points of agreement; minimize disagreements. Draw attention to the objective at hand.<br><br>Pose a direct question to an uninvolved member on the topic.<br><br>As a last resort, frankly state that personalities should be left out of the discussion. |
| Wrong Track | Brings up ideas that are obviously incorrect | Tactfully make any corrections or solicit someone else's opinion to help convey the correct information to the group.<br><br>Say "I see your point, but can we reconcile that with our current situation?"<br><br>Remember, all group members will hear how you respond to this individual. Your response will either encourage or discourage future participation, so be tactful. |
| Quiet One | Bored, indifferent, timid, or superior | Gain interest by asking for their opinion.<br><br>Question the person next to them. Then ask the quiet one to comment on the view expressed.<br><br>Compliment this person the first time they contribute. Be sincere.<br><br>Indicate respect for this person's experience, then ask for ideas. |
| Bungler | Lacks the ability to put good ideas into proper order; needs help to convey ideas | Don't call attention to the problem. Say "Let me see if I understand what you are saying," then repeat the ideas more clearly. |

STEP 7

| Behavior | Why It Happens | What to Do |
|---|---|---|
| Mule | Can't or won't see the other side; supports own viewpoint no matter what | Ask other members of the group to comment on their ideas. They will straighten them out.<br><br>Remind them that time is short and suggest that they accept the group consensus presently. Indicate your willingness to talk with them later, then follow up. |
| Talker | Highly motivated, show-off, well informed, or just plain talkative | Slow this person down with some difficult questions.<br><br>Say "That's an interesting point. Now let's see what the rest think about it."<br><br>Draw on their knowledge, but relay to the group.<br><br>In general, for all overly talkative folks, let the group take care of them as much as possible. |
| Griper | Has a pet peeve, gripes for the sake of complaining, or has a legitimate complaint | Point out that the objective at hand is to operate as efficiently and cooperatively as possible under the present circumstances.<br><br>Indicate that you will discuss the personal problems privately at a later date.<br><br>Have another member of the group respond to the complaint. |

In general, facilitator tactics for handling disruptive behavior should include:

- avoiding one-on-one power struggles
- remaining unbiased, calm, and unemotional
- helping participants define the facts, the supporting evidence, and any assumptions
- using good-natured humor

STEP 7

- asking for clarification, or summarizing the issue to confirm
- connecting with the participant on a personal level
- broadening the participation of the rest of the group
- protecting participants as needed using a separate parking lot to postpone issues until they are appropriate for discussion
- recognizing the individual's point and then either gaining the viewpoints of others or taking the discussion offline
- creating a safe environment for discussion.

## The Next Step

Many meetings today take place virtually, rather than in-person. The next chapter outlines the many benefits of this ever-progressing technology as well as the unique challenges a virtual facilitator faces.

STEP 7

# Step 8
# Facilitate Virtually

## Overview

- Distinguish between in-person and virtual meetings.
- Master the virtual tools and technology.
- Communicate virtually.

Virtual meetings allow groups to collaborate who might otherwise never have the chance, most likely because their locations make travel to in-person meetings too expensive and time consuming. Thankfully, technology provides a way for teams to work together remotely and accomplish much of the same work.

The facilitator of a virtual meeting—whether working via video or web conference, or audio only—has much the same role as the facilitator of an in-person meeting, with some advantages and disadvantages. Virtual meetings save money on time and expenses moving people from place to place and paying for the use of an off-site meeting place or food and beverages. But virtual meetings do have shortcomings. Most obviously, because people are not in the same room together, communication becomes more difficult; it's harder for people to build rapport with one another, and easier for people to become distracted and disengage from the meeting. Plus, there's more room for technical error. For these reasons, the facilitator's job is as important as ever. To do it well, you must begin by understanding the differences between in-person and virtual meetings.

STEP
8

# Distinguish Between In-Person and Virtual Meetings

At its essence, a virtual meeting is still a gathering of a group of people to accomplish a specific goal. Most of the concerns for understanding your role as a facilitator are the same: preparing for the meeting, beginning the meeting, helping the group generate ideas and make decisions, integrating media and technology, maximizing learning and participation, keeping the meeting on track, and dealing with conflict.

## Extra Considerations for Facilitating Virtually

When getting ready to facilitate a virtual session, keep the following in mind:

### Arrive Early

Even though it's a virtual session, the facilitator should still be the first to arrive at the meeting, preferably at least 30 minutes early. (If the meeting software charges by the minute, talk to your client about the necessity of the extra time.) Make sure the meeting software is working correctly and documents have been uploaded so you can be available to chat with any other early arrivers. Use the time for casual conversation, to establish rapport with participants, and to help them warm up with each other.

### Begin the Meeting on Time

Begin on time, no matter the number of participants who have arrived. As with in-person meetings, this sets the tone that participants are expected to be punctual.

### Open With an Icebreaker

Especially for groups that have never met in person, taking a few minutes to get to know each other will pay off; participants will feel more comfortable speaking and will be more likely to speak up throughout the day. See step 3 for examples of acquainters you can use in virtual meetings.

## Lay the Groundwork

Agree on the meeting outcomes, review the agenda, introduce the parking lot, and establish ground rules. While many of the ground rules for in-person meetings apply, be sure to consider some specific to virtual meetings, including:

- Say your name each time you speak.
- Keep comments focused and short.
- No multitasking.
- Determine whether to ban the "mute" button. While "mute" does cut down on background noise, it can also increase the likelihood of people multitasking. Mute also cuts out natural forms of communication like laughter and quick reactions to comments, which are important for positive group dynamics.

## Keep Presentations to a Minimum

While this is important for in-person meetings, it's more so for virtual meetings, where people are more likely to get bored and disengage.

## Design Meetings for Interaction

Activities for virtual meetings don't just have to be discussions. Meeting software typically includes tools for groups to whiteboard, share documents, and even enter "breakout rooms" together.

STEP **8**

## Take Regular Breaks

Even though you're not in the same room together, people still need to stand up, stretch, get a snack, or use the restroom. If the meeting runs longer than 90 minutes, make sure to schedule regular five- or 10-minute breaks, preferably once an hour after the first 90 minutes. This will also allow people to check their email or make a quick phone call, reducing the temptation to multitask during the meeting.

## Summarize Accomplishments

Finally, when the meeting is over, summarize accomplishments, next steps, and action items, including dates and people responsible, just as you would in an in-person meeting.

While virtual meetings can be just as effective as in-person meetings, it's important to acknowledge the differences and account for them. Let's look at some additional concerns you should consider specifically when facilitating a virtual meeting.

## Share Technical Information

The meeting invitation should include not only the day, time, time zone, agenda, and goals of the meeting, it must also contain the instructions for people to log in or dial in and, if necessary, any technical requirements such as bandwidth or software downloads.

## Choose Your Own Physical Location

You have to find your own physical meeting space. As the facilitator, you should have a quiet room, preferably one with a door that closes. Encourage participants to also find a quiet room, such as a conference room or home office, that can be used during the meeting. You need a place that's as distraction-free as an in-person meeting environment would be, perhaps even more so, since virtual meetings require additional concentration and focus to remain engaged. The coffee shop that's empty at 6:45 a.m. may be a circus by 9 a.m., so choose wisely.

## Become a Technical Expert

It's important for the participants to feel comfortable with the virtual meeting tools, but it's critical for the facilitator. If you're using a new meeting platform, spend as much time as possible becoming familiar with it before the day of the meeting. Take advantage of any tutorials or training. Even if it's a platform you've used many times before, double check that your equipment is working, any required software is up to date, all documents and visual aids have been uploaded and are available for participants, and that tools such as whiteboards, chat, and breakout rooms are functioning.

## Host an Orientation for the Participants

Invite participants to make sure they can log in at least 24 hours beforehand, so any technical difficulties can be resolved before the start of the meeting. This is also a good time for participants to play with the tools the platform offers so they can begin to feel comfortable using them.

### Identify Technical Support People

Most likely, you will be viewed not only as meeting facilitator but as technical support for the inevitable problems people will have connecting and participating in the meeting. Provide contact information for at least one person who can deliver technical support during the facilitation session, since it would not be fair to the group for you to stop the meeting and resolve their issues.

### If Possible, Keep the Group Small

Because communication is more difficult in a virtual meeting, it's better to keep the size of the group down so that people can have a chance to speak up and try to become familiar with one another, which takes more effort when you're not in the same place physically. With smaller groups—typically fewer than eight people—you have more options for videoconferencing, including the ability to see everyone on one screen at the same time. This enables nonverbal communication such as eye contact, facial expressions, and hand gestures, all important in establishing healthy group dynamics. Smaller groups also encounter less "social loafing," a term that describes individuals in a group allowing others to do the work while they reduce their effort, according to Mark de Rond (2012), author of *There Is an I in Team*.

### Decide Whether You Want to Record the Session

Most virtual conferencing tools allow you to record the audio, visual, or both. It might be helpful to have a record of ideas and decisions; it may also help those auditory learners in your group to listen to the recording at a later date, or save the recording for anyone who was unable to attend the meeting. However, if sensitive or confidential information is discussed, it may be better not to record. Check with the meeting client to see whether the company requires a recording.

STEP 8

## Master Virtual Tools and Technology

Just as visual aids can enhance in-person sessions, an ever-expanding menu of tools can increase collaboration and engagement for your virtual meeting. As you plan your session, learn which tools are available through your virtual meeting software. The following are a few examples to look for.

### Screen Sharing

This feature allows you to display your computer screen to all of the participants. When other users select the "shared screen" option, they can see a view of your monitor almost exactly as it appears in front of you, with only minor differences in formatting. This is vital for sharing important visual information.

### File Sharing

This feature allows you to share the agenda and other meeting materials instantly. Most also include tools that allow you or participants to mark up documents onscreen.

### Virtual Chat

Chat is one of the most common features in virtual meetings; similar to text messaging on cell phones, it's one of the simplest ways to increase interaction among participants. Chat can be private between facilitator and a participant, private between one or more participants, or public for the whole group. If a meeting software doesn't have breakout rooms, the chat function can be used for small group discussions or brainstorming. Private messages also let participants tell the facilitator when they have a question, an idea for later discussion, a technical problem, or any other concern.

Chat functions appeal to different learning preferences, including verbal and intrapersonal learners. Find out whether your software offers chat functions, options for chatting between individuals and groups, and whether transcripts of chats (public or private) are available.

### Shared Whiteboards

Whiteboards and flipcharts are two of the most common and useful facilitation tools for in-person meetings—used to post the agenda, the goals and deliverables for the meeting, items for the parking lot, and important points and ideas as the meeting progresses—and they are no less useful in a virtual meeting. Virtual whiteboards typically give the facilitator and participants the ability to write in a space visible to all—usually with a variety of colored fonts and markup tools, and the ability to upload and post documents to be seen by all.

Often the group can have multiple whiteboards, or multiple people can write on one whiteboard at once, which is useful for brainstorming activities. The interactive whiteboard can be called up in a separate window, which you or any participant can write or draw on freely with the results visible to all participants.

### Breakout Rooms

Small group activities are a component of almost every meeting, and, thanks to technology, can also be a productive part of virtual meetings. Breakout rooms are different from chat for several reasons. For one thing, participants within the small group, or breakout room, can speak to one another through their headset or computer microphone. Participants also have access to collaboration tools, such as virtual whiteboards and file sharing, reserved for just their group. The facilitator can move between breakout rooms, assist where needed, and move on to the next group, just as they would with in-person meetings.

STEP 8

Spend some time with your meeting software to learn more about how breakout rooms operate, including how you can assign participants to breakout rooms and whether you can do it ahead of time (again, allowing participants time to practice "moving" to these small groups). Also find out whether whiteboards or other documents created in breakout rooms can be brought back into the main group conference and shared with the entire group.

### Screen Monitoring

Many platforms allow the facilitator to see who is participating, typically by indicating whether participants are looking at the video conferencing window or have another window open on their laptop (indicating they're working on something else). This function can sometimes also tell the facilitator whether a participant has engaged in any way within a certain amount of time (for example, the past 10 minutes). Let participants know if you plan to use this function; it will increase their participation and reduce feelings of being spied on.

### Synchronized Web Browsing

This feature allows the group to browse a website together, for example to learn more about a client or competitor, to do research together, or to discuss design ideas for a new website.

### Surveys and Polls

These tools can easily be built into a virtual meeting ahead of time and used for decision making, or can be created in the moment to take the pulse of the group. When using surveys and polls, participants usually want to see the results immediately. To save time, arrange polls with predefined answers (rather than having participants write free-form comments). Try to find out whether you can share individual results and aggregate results with the group, whether you can create polls or surveys spontaneously during a meeting, whether results can be displayed anonymously, and whether you can export the data to spreadsheets for analysis.

### Session Recording and Reporting

If possible, record your live sessions and meetings for quality control or archiving. Publish your recordings to your group or give individual playback permissions. Many virtual meeting platforms also offer sophisticated reporting features, providing a record of who attended, their engagement, and transcripts of chats. You should also be able to export reports in forms that interface with your customer relationship management (CRM) systems.

### Closed Captioning for the Hearing Impaired

Closed captioning lets hearing impaired participants follow spoken communication, typically from both the facilitator and other participants.

### Support for Multilanguage Audiences

Interface text may be available in languages other than English. Additionally, translator features may be available similar to a closed-caption function, which may enable participants to read the facilitator's words on their screens in their preferred language.

**POINTER**

If possible, choose a virtual conference tool that employs video, rather than just audio. While you might not always be able to see everyone, especially if you must look at documents or a whiteboard together, any amount of time spent looking at each other helps build team rapport. You will also be much more likely to have the undivided attention of the participants if they know you can see them.

STEP 8

# Communicate Virtually

Communication is potentially the biggest obstacle for virtual teams. Healthy group dynamics are difficult enough when people are in the same room, and they're even more difficult when participants are merely voices on a telephone, or, at best, a face on a video screen—not to mention additional barriers of geography, time zones, language, and culture that so often are involved with virtual teams.

As a facilitator, you must work harder to bridge communication gaps, make sure everyone has a chance to speak and be heard, and make sure everyone has the same understanding of the original problem, the goals of the meeting, developed ideas, and the range of solutions. Consider the following tips to keep communication healthy and productive.

## Use ELMOs (Enough, Let's Move On)

ELMO is an easy and lighthearted way to keep things moving. If everyone is on camera, ask that the person holds up a piece of paper that says ELMO and then respectfully give the current speaker time to wrap up (one minute or less). If you use ELMO, establish this communication method during the ground rules and make sure everyone agrees on how it should be used. The idea isn't to shut anyone down, but to have a way to gently ask if the group can move on.

### Overcommunicate

Especially at the beginning of the meeting, it's better to overcommunicate the goals of the meeting to make sure everyone is on the same page. Ask questions to the group as you go along to check and double check you all have the same understanding.

### Offer Suggestions, Not Critiques

It's easier for communication to be perceived as negative and to allow conflict to settle in during a virtual meeting, when everyone has less of a sense of each other's nonverbal cues. When discussing ideas and solutions, ask everyone to frame their points as "suggestions" rather than critiques on someone else's specific point.

### Make Sure Everyone Gets a Chance to Speak

As a facilitator, rather than scanning the room for quiet participants, you'll likely have to scan a list of participants to see who hasn't yet contributed. Make sure everyone is speaking to make sure everyone is engaged, rather than playing solitaire or doing other work.

STEP 8

## Establish Back Channels

If you're using a platform that allows everyone to see each other's faces, the facilitator and other participants can see if someone wants to speak (for example, raising their hand, taking a breath, leaning forward) or if someone is bored (rolling eyes, glazed look). If you do not have everyone on camera, establish a back channel for each participant to be able to communicate with you directly. In many virtual meeting platforms, participants "raise their hands" (clicking a button alerts the facilitator that a hand is raised, showing up as an icon on the facilitator's screen), or type a question or comment to you directly, either with or without the rest of the group viewing. When you get a question or comment, acknowledge it, whether or not you can answer the question or address the concern immediately. A simple, "OK, thanks" lets the person know you received the message.

## Have a Method for Participants to Answer Questions

Posing a question to the entire group is easier during an in-person meeting rather than a virtual one. In an in-person meeting, everyone can see each other and understand who is about to speak. In virtual meetings, you may have 10 seconds of silence followed by three people talking at once, followed by another 20 seconds of awkward exchanges of "No, go ahead." Methods may include the facilitator calling on someone directly, or asking participants to raise their hands (either visually or via a back channel). Again, these methods should be covered when establishing ground rules. If, as the facilitator, you elect to call on someone, also establish that that person has the option to pass. This will diminish anxiety of being called on if the participant doesn't want to reply.

STEP **8**

## Follow Up With Participants

Follow up, either as a group or individually, to thank participants for their contributions and see if they have any further questions or concerns. This helps reinforce that there is a human at the other end of the virtual meeting, rather than letting participants feel they're lost in cyberspace.

### Use Feedback Tools

To offset the nonverbal communication that comes so easily with in-person meetings, consider using polls, surveys, and other feedback tools (such as the ones discussed in the previous section) throughout the meeting to keep participants engaged. These tools can help the facilitator understand whether everyone understands the issues at hand, if the group is going too fast or too slow, or if the group is approaching a consensus or not. Many survey tools can also be used anonymously, which might increase honesty and candid feedback.

Virtual meetings are an excellent option for teams that otherwise might never get to work together. While the technology will no doubt continue to evolve, people—and their need to connect personally, communicate clearly, and achieve satisfaction in accomplishing goals—will continue to benefit from effective facilitation. Use the checklist in Tool 8-1 to keep track of how you need to prepare before a virtual facilitation session.

## TOOL 8-1
### VIRTUAL FACILITATION CHECKLIST

Use this checklist to ensure you are prepared, and that you have prepared the participants, for your virtual meeting. Supplement this list with the checklist in step 2.

**Two or More Weeks Before the Meeting (Start as Soon as Possible)**

- ❑ Send out a meeting request, including dial-in or log-in instructions and any technical requirements. Remember to indicate the time zone in which the meeting is set.
- ❑ Send requests for any pre-work and any necessary materials to participants.
- ❑ Make a list of all supporting materials that you need (including uploaded documents, web addresses, and any hardware you may need, such as noise-canceling headphones or a high quality microphone).

### One Week Before the Facilitation Session

❑ Identify a quiet location, preferably a room with a door, to use on the day of the meeting.

❑ Identify a technical support contact who will be available during the meeting; if possible, email their contact information to the participants.

❑ Confirm that participants have received the meeting invitation and any necessary technical information.

❑ Practice the facilitation session, including logging in and using all of the meeting features, such as setting up and writing on whiteboards, moving to different breakout rooms, and ensuring all of the communication back channels are functioning properly. Enlist the help of a colleague, if possible, to pose as a participant and make sure you can communicate with them properly.

❑ Offer a scheduled orientation where participants can informally check their connections and software are working correctly and can play with the tools (whiteboards, chat rooms, and so on).

❑ Prepare surveys and polls to be used during the meeting.

### Meeting Day

❑ Arrive at least 30 minutes prior to the facilitation session time.

❑ Test all equipment, especially the sound.

❑ Prepare to record the session, if preferred. Make sure to tell all participants that the session is being recorded.

### Before You Begin the Facilitation Session

❑ Review the first 90 seconds of your opening.

❑ Do deep breathing and stretch techniques to help you relax.

❑ Greet participants.

## The Next Step

The next step outlines ways to bring the meeting, whether in-person or virtually, to a close.

# Step 9

# Close the Meeting and Follow Up

## Overview

- Plan effective closing activities.
- Debrief the meeting.
- Follow up after the meeting.

The end of a facilitation session is usually what participants remember most, so it is important to make the ending a memorable one. Without proper closure, the outcome and next steps of the meeting can be unclear and potentially sour a meeting, which was, up until that point, effective. Each agenda point should be deliberately closed by checking for group alignment on accomplishments and next steps, and asking the group whether anyone has any additional questions or comments.

## Plan Effective Closing Activities

Schedule time in the agenda for a closing activity. The length of time required for this segment of the facilitation session depends on the length of the session itself. For example, a four-hour facilitation session may have a 15-minute closing activity, whereas a two-day session may require an hour for the close. A good closing activity should accomplish the following:

### Keep It Positive

Highlight accomplishments and thank the group for their work and their time. Even if the group had a few hurdles, some sincere recognition from the facilitator can frame the meeting as constructive and help the group leave on an optimistic note.

### Review and Summarize

Take a few minutes to summarize and review what was covered during the session, including consensus points and goals accomplished. Go over the agenda points and indicate what you covered, what was not covered, and any possible items for another meeting.

### Discuss Outstanding Questions

Allow at least five minutes of question time at the end of the session summary to ensure that everyone has the same perception of the meeting as you do and there are no points of confusion.

### Gain Agreement From Participants and Clarify Next Steps

End the session by gaining group consensus on the contents and outcomes of the meeting. Summarize any action items or next steps, or, if necessary, schedule future meetings, whether in person or virtual. Each action item should be assigned to a specific person and have a specific delivery date. Make sure there's some form of accountability to confirm the task is getting done. Never end a session with a vague, "I'll get back in touch with the action items we discussed!" Make those clear before anyone leaves the meeting; make sure the participants agree with the course of action.

### Evaluate the Session

Distribute an evaluation form to maintain and improve the facilitation session quality (learn more on session evaluation in step 10).

### End on Time and Thank Participants

Close the meeting on time or better yet, a few minutes early to show that you respect the participants' time. If there are agenda points that did not get covered, plan to have another meeting. Then, never forget to leave participants with a sincere thank you for their time and participation.

## Debrief the Meeting

A debrief session should be included as the primary closing activity. A debrief is a short conversation about what went well and what did not go well within the meeting. The practice of debriefing after each meeting, or any major portion of the agenda, ensures all participants are on the same page about what has been discussed or accomplished. Debriefing should take place at the end of the event and should be quick and honest.

First, explain the purpose of the debrief to the group and why it will benefit them. Led by the facilitator, participants take turns discussing the meeting content, as well as what worked and what didn't work about the meeting processes. Because these conversations can be used to improve future meetings, encourage all participants to be honest and forthright. It may be helpful to use the agenda as a map, walking through each objective and determining whether the group and facilitator met the expectations. Walking through the agenda also helps keep the group focused on what they were supposed to accomplish, rather than allowing the debrief to dissolve into a rambling conversation of additional ideas or complaints.

If the participants are tired or not quick to engage in the debrief, get the conversation going by asking open-ended questions. Questions can be about the objectives and accomplishments within the meeting, about how well the meeting processes worked, or about next steps. Questions may include:

- What are your initial thoughts about what we just completed?
- What was the highlight of the day for you?
- What was the low point?
- How was the process of finding a consensus?
- How can we do a better job of keeping the meeting on track next time?

STEP **9**

Or ask each participant to complete a sentence, such as:

- The most effective part of the day was . . .
- I can offer support by . . .
- I need additional support for . . .

**POINTER**

If possible, set aside a few minutes of your debriefing time to allow everyone 30 seconds of uninterrupted time to offer their final thoughts. Don't let this become a conversation or debate—just one last chance for everyone to be heard. If you don't have enough time, consider asking participants to sum up their day in one word.

As the facilitator, plan to comment on what you believe went well and any areas for possible improvement in the next meeting. As with discussions throughout the day, the ground rules apply, meaning no one should suffer an attack for offering their honest feedback. Consider adding one additional rule for this activity: asking participants not to comment on others' remarks, in order to keep the debrief within the set time limits and to prevent a descent into repeating discussions from earlier in the day. Remind participants to keep feedback focused on the accomplishments and processes of the day, rather than on any team members. If possible, capture responses on a flipchart and use them to understand how the group can work more effectively next time.

Debriefing is important but won't happen unless it has its own place on the meeting's agenda. Debriefing can easily be pushed aside to make room for longer discussions or to allow everyone to depart after a long day, but the end of the meeting is at least as important as the beginning. Don't shortcut this step.

## Follow Up After the Meeting

With the meeting nearly at a close, what's a facilitator to do—pack up and leave? Not quite. In fact, follow-up on action items is mission-critical for the group to continue to make progress toward the goals outside of meeting hours. At the close of a meeting, don't forget to:

Remain available to the participants. Encourage them to email you with additional questions
or comments; if your role with this group will not
continue, forward the emails to your client or the
appropriate person. The purpose is to create an
open line of communication to keep important
conversations going.

**POINTER**

Try to stand by the
door and shake
everyone's hand
as they leave. Look
each person in
the eye and thank
them for their
participation.

Type up clear and concise notes from the meeting and distribute as soon as possible, preferably
within a few days. Make sure that everyone who
attended the meeting receives a copy as well as anyone affected by the
outcomes of the meeting who did not attend.

Follow up on commitments. If you said that you were going to
do something, make sure that you do it in a timely manner! If your
association with this group ends after the meeting, assign one person
to be accountable for each action item, and set clear deadlines for the
action. Plan a follow-up meeting to make sure that commitments are
being upheld and the purpose of the meeting is achieved. Follow-up
meetings often point out if any new problems have surfaced that
meeting participants need to solve.

## The Next Step

Once you've brought the meeting to a close and prepared any
follow-up as necessary, your job is not over quite yet. What went
right? What went wrong? Does the group have any suggested
improvements for you as a facilitator? The final step focuses on how
you can evaluate your performance in order to continue your professional development.

STEP
**9**

# Step 10

# Evaluate the Facilitation Session

## Overview

- Conduct a self-evaluation.
- Have the group critique itself.
- Have the group evaluate the facilitator.
- Have a trained observer conduct the evaluation.

The last step in the process of successful facilitation is to evaluate what worked and what did not. Given the amount of time that people spend in meetings, isn't it surprising how seldom the effectiveness of a meeting is evaluated?

Keep in mind that the point of evaluating a facilitation session is to allow continuous improvement, both for the specific group of participants and the organization as a whole. Evaluations help measure how well the group met its objectives, how well the meeting processes worked, and how well the individual participants functioned as a group. The evaluation process can happen on several levels—for example, you may critique yourself, have the group critique itself, and have the group provide feedback about your skills as a facilitator; you may even have a trained observer attend the facilitation session with the sole purpose of providing you with expert feedback.

Let's look at each evaluation option and some suggestions on how to gather the feedback.

## Conduct a Self-Evaluation

After the meeting ends, you can reflect on the meeting and how reality compared with what you planned. (This is another reason why planning the facilitation session is so important: if you don't have a plan going in, what are you going to evaluate yourself against?) When conducting a self-evaluation, be careful to be objective and evaluate what happened from an outsider's perspective. The goal is improvement for future meetings! To facilitate this process, consider using the tool shown in Tool 10-1.

### TOOL 10-1
### FACILITATOR SELF-EVALUATION

**Objectives**
- What were the meeting objectives?
- Were they accomplished?    ❑ Yes    ❑ No    ❑ Not Sure
- Which objectives were not completely accomplished? Why not? (Be specific.)

**Processes**
- If I were conducting the meeting again, what would I do the same? What would I do differently?

| | Same | Different | Comments |
|---|---|---|---|
| Location | | | |
| Scheduled time | | | |
| Selection of participants | | | |
| Objectives | | | |
| Room setup | | | |

| | Same | Different | Comments |
|---|---|---|---|
| Audiovisual aids | | | |
| Agenda | | | |
| My own preparation | | | |
| Advance notice to participants | | | |
| Introduction | | | |
| Amount of participation from the group | | | |
| Conclusion | | | |
| What else would I do differently? | | | |

- Were objectives accomplished in minimum time?
  ❐ Yes   ❐ No   ❐ Not Sure
- If objectives were not accomplished in minimum time, why not? (Be specific.)

**Participants**

- In your opinion, how satisfied were participants with the meeting?
  ❐ Very Satisfied   ❐ Satisfied   ❐ Dissatisfied   ❐ Very Dissatisfied

Beyond the evaluation of one particular meeting, work to become an effective facilitator, honing your skills by strengthening your major weaknesses. Successful facilitators continually develop themselves by reading, attending seminars or workshops, tackling challenging job assignments, coaching, and so on. Use Tool 10-2 to continue to develop your skills in creating and leading productive meetings.

STEP 10

## TOOL 10-2
### FACILITATOR STRENGTHS AND WEAKNESSES

**Instructions:**

- Describe one strength you want to hone and one weakness you want to overcome.
- Identify the method for development and the resources it requires.
- Establish a timeline for your development activities.
- Determine the required feedback so you can gauge the extent of your improvement.

**Describe One Strength**

| Method for Development | Resources | Timeline | Feedback |
|---|---|---|---|
|  |  |  |  |

**Describe One Weakness**

| Method for Development | Resources | Timeline | Feedback |
|---|---|---|---|
|  |  |  |  |

*Used with permission from McCain (2015).*

# Have the Group Critique Itself

One way to have a group learn from experience is by critiquing its own success during or at the conclusion of a meeting. For example, you can post a flipchart with one half labeled "What we did well" and the other half labeled "What we need to improve." Ask participants to reflect on the meeting and to help complete the flipchart.

Many of these ideas may be incorporated into future meetings or may be found on a growing list of ground rules as the group figures out how to efficiently work together.

## Have the Group Evaluate the Facilitator

Group members can provide a wealth of evaluation information. Keep in mind that many of the meeting participants may not be objective when providing feedback during the evaluation process—but nonetheless, they are a valuable source of information on how to improve future meetings.

Depending on the type of meeting, different evaluation forms might be most helpful to capture feedback anonymously. For example, some focus on the venue and logistics, others may focus on how successfully the group accomplished its objectives, what participants learned, the quality of activities, or the applicability to their job roles. In general, consider using these guidelines to get honest, meaningful reactions to all types of meetings:

**POINTER**

Identify the type of information that you want to receive feedback on (for example, agenda topics, facilitation skills, room setup, visual aids, activities, and so on) and then craft the evaluation form to match the input you seek.

- Determine what kind of information you want (agenda topics, facilitation skills, room setup and facilities, handouts, visual aids, number and type of activities to engage the group and keep them involved, and so on).
- Prepare a written form to get reactions from the participants.
- Design the form so that the information can be tabulated and quantified. Rather than open-ended questions like "How well did you like the program?" or "What did you like best?" ask, "On a scale from one to five, how effective was our meeting (with five being most effective)?"
- If possible, prepare the survey using an online tool. Results can be quickly tabulated and analyzed this way. It's best to ask participants to complete the survey before they leave

the meeting, so they will need access to the Internet and a computer or their smartphone. Participants can also be asked to complete the survey at another time, although the response rate will likely drop dramatically.

- Allow participants to add comments that will help explain their reactions and offer suggestions for improvement. A good question is, "What would have made the meeting more effective?" or "How could the meeting have been improved?"
- Obtain honest reactions by removing any fear of repercussions for negative comments. The best way to do this is to make the forms anonymous. Have participants leave the completed forms on a table on their way out of the room, or, if using an online survey tool, do not ask for names or email addresses.

**POINTER**

Although they might not be entirely objective, individual participants serve as a good source of information on how to improve future facilitation sessions.

## Have a Trained Observer Conduct the Evaluation

Having a trained observer sit quietly in the back of the room and objectively observe the facilitation session can provide helpful evaluation information for improvement. A trained observer can be anyone who understands the characteristics of an effective meeting, such as an experienced facilitator who is recognized for successful meetings.

Depending on the type of meeting, you might want the observer to focus on certain aspects of the session or your skills and jot down general notes on a pad of paper. Or, to gather more formal feedback, perhaps have the observer complete a form as observations are made during the session.

When having a trained observer evaluate your facilitation sessions, consider using a form similar to Tool 10-3 to systematically gather formal feedback in specific areas. But most important, be receptive to comments from the trained observer. Don't be defensive—the trained observer's goal is to help you improve future meetings.

## POINTER

Do not be afraid of evaluation—gathering and reflecting on feedback will help you continually improve and hone your skills as a facilitator.

## TOOL 10-3
### EVALUATION BY A TRAINED OBSERVER

| | Poor | Fair | Good | Very Good | Excellent |
|---|---|---|---|---|---|
| **Statement of Objectives** | | | | | |

Comment:

| | Poor | Fair | Good | Very Good | Excellent |
|---|---|---|---|---|---|
| **Presentation Effectiveness** | | | | | |

Comment:

| | Poor | Fair | Good | Very Good | Excellent |
|---|---|---|---|---|---|
| **Ratio of Presentation to Participation** | | | | | |

Comment:

| | Poor | Fair | Good | Very Good | Excellent |
|---|---|---|---|---|---|
| **Control of the Meeting** | | | | | |

Comment:

| | Poor | Fair | Good | Very Good | Excellent |
|---|---|---|---|---|---|
| **Use of Visual Aids** | | | | | |

Comment:

STEP 10

## EVALUATION BY A TRAINED OBSERVER (CONT.)

| | Poor | Fair | Good | Very Good | Excellent |
|---|---|---|---|---|---|
| **Use of Technology** | | | | | |

Comment:

| | Poor | Fair | Good | Very Good | Excellent |
|---|---|---|---|---|---|
| **Effectiveness of Group Involvement** | | | | | |

Comment:

| | Poor | Fair | Good | Very Good | Excellent |
|---|---|---|---|---|---|
| **Conclusion of Meeting** | | | | | |

Comment:

| | Poor | Fair | Good | Very Good | Excellent |
|---|---|---|---|---|---|
| **Overall Effectiveness** | | | | | |

Comment:

| | Poor | Fair | Good | Very Good | Excellent |
|---|---|---|---|---|---|
| **Suggestions for Improvement** | | | | | |

Comment:

| **Physical Facilities** | Poor | Fair | Good | Very Good | Excellent |
|---|---|---|---|---|---|
| Room Setup | | | | | |
| Temperature | | | | | |
| Quiet | | | | | |
| Comfort | | | | | |
| Ventilation | | | | | |

| **Introduction** | | | | | |
|---|---|---|---|---|---|
| Start on time | | | | | |
| Create interest and attention | | | | | |
| Clarify objectives | | | | | |

STEP **10**

| | Poor | Fair | Good | Very Good | Excellent |
|---|---|---|---|---|---|
| **Main Body** | | | | | |
| Information clearly presented | | | | | |
| Ratio of presentation to discussion | | | | | |
| **Audiovisual Aids** | | | | | |
| Selection | | | | | |
| Use | | | | | |
| **Other** | | | | | |
| Attitude of facilitator toward group | | | | | |
| Maintenance of interest and enthusiasm | | | | | |
| Handling of people problems (e.g., tangents or dominating conversations) | | | | | |
| Control of meeting | | | | | |
| **Conclusion** | | | | | |
| Summary of meeting, decisions, and next steps | | | | | |
| Accomplishment of objectives | | | | | |
| Final comments and assignments | | | | | |
| **End Meeting on Time** | | | | | |

STEP 10

No matter which evaluation techniques you decide to employ (the more the better!), some sort of evaluation should be conducted at the end of each facilitation session in an effort to capitalize on what went well and to diminish or eliminate the less-than-desirable occurrences. That's how skilled facilitators continue to hone and perfect their skills in specific areas to become truly successful.

# References

Adams, T., J. Means, and M. Spivey. 2015. *The Project Meeting Facilitator: Facilitation Skills to Make the Most of Project Meetings.* Hoboken, NJ: John Wiley & Sons.

Bens, I. 2017. *Facilitating With Ease! Core Skills for Facilitators, Team Leaders and Members, Managers, Consultants and Training,* 4th ed. Hoboken, NJ: John Wiley & Sons.

Callahan, M., and C. Russo, eds. 1999. "10 Great Games and How to Use Them." *Infoline.* Alexandria, VA: ASTD Press.

Cassidy, M. 1999. "Group Decision Making." *Infoline.* Alexandria, VA: ASTD Press.

Darraugh, B. 1997. "Group Process Tools." *Infoline.* Alexandria, VA: ASTD Press.

de Rond, M. 2012. "Why Less Is More in Teams." *Harvard Business Review*, August 6. https://hbr.org/2012/08/why-less-is-more-in-teams.

Devlin, K. 2017. *Facilitation Skills Training.* Alexandria, VA: ATD Press.

Downs, L. 2016. *Time Management Training.* Alexandria, VA: ATD Press.

Estep, T. 2005. "Meetings that Work!" *Infoline.* Alexandria, VA: ASTD Press.

Finkel, C., and A. Finkel. 2000. "Facilities Planning." *Infoline.* Alexandria, VA: ASTD Press.

Gardner, H. 1983. *Frames of Mind: The Theory of Multiple Intelligences.* New York: Basic Books.

Haines, R. 2014. "Group Development in Virtual Teams: An Experimental Reexamination." *Computers in Human Behavior* 39:213-222.

Hugget, C. 2018. *Virtual Training Basics,* 2nd ed. Alexandria, VA: ATD Press.

Johnson, S.R. 2018. *Engaging the Workplace: Using Surveys to Spark Change.* Alexandria, VA: ATD Press.

Kirkpatrick, D. 2006. *How to Conduct Productive Meetings.* Alexandria, VA: ASTD Press.

Ludwig, D., and G. Owen-Boger. 2017. *Effective SMEs: A Trainer's Guide for Helping Subject Matter Experts Facilitate Learning.* Alexandria, VA: ATD Press.

McCain, D. 2015. *Facilitation Basics,* 2nd ed. Alexandria, VA: ATD Press.

Palmer, E. 2017. *Own Any Occasion: Mastering the Art of Speaking and Presenting.* Alexandria, VA: ATD Press.

Parker, P. 2018. *The Art of Gathering: How We Meet and Why It Matters.* New York: Riverhead Books.

Piskurich, G. 2002. *HPI Essentials.* Alexandria, VA: ASTD Press.

Rosania, R.J. 2003. *Presentation Basics.* Alexandria, VA: ASTD Press.

Russo, C.S. 2000. "Storytelling." *Infoline.* Alexandria, VA: ASTD Press.

Spruell, G. 1997. "More Productive Meetings." *Infoline.* Alexandria, VA: ASTD Press.

Steffey, D. 2017. *Destination Facilitation: A Travel Guide to Training Around the World.* Alexandria, VA: ATD Press.

Tuckman, B., and M.A. Jensen. 1997. "Stages of Small Group Development Revisited." *Group and Organizational Studies* 4:419-427.

Walton, A.P., and M. Kemmelmeier. 2012. "Creativity in Its Social Context: The Interplay of Organizational Norms, Situational Threat, and Gender." *Creativity Research Journal* 24(2-3): 208-219.

# Index

humor, 101
hypothetical questions, 98

## I

icebreakers
    acquainters, 41–45
    openers, 40–41, 132
idea generation
    affinity diagramming, 59–61
    anonymous suggestions, 54–55
    brainwriting, 55
    fish bone diagramming, 57–58
    ground rules, 53
    mind mapping, 56–57
    multivoting (nominal group technique), 61–62
    reverse brainstorming, 62
    round robins, 54
    SCAMPER, 64–65
    Six Thinking Hats, 66
    spectrum listening, 62
    storyboarding, 63–64
    tools, 52–53
interactivity levels associated with different media tool, 79
internal *vs.* external facilitators, 11–12
Internet
    streaming media, 85–87
interpersonal learning style, 21
interpersonal tips for keeping on track, 95
interrelationship diagramming, 59–61
interruptions
    guidelines for the facilitator, 121–122
    timing, 121
    types of mediations, 121
intrapersonal learning style, 21
Ishikawa diagram, 57–58
"I" statements, 124

## J

Jensen, Mary Jane, 112
jitters, reducing, 33

## K

keeping on track
    facilitation tips tool, 92–93
    interpersonal tips, 95
    knowing how and when to intervene, 91–93, 109–110, 119, 125
    participation tips, 94
    schedule tips, 93–94
    in virtual meetings, 95
Kemmelmeier, Markus, 53

## L

language
    multi-language audiences, 139
    using precise, 67–68
learning styles
    about, 19–20
    addressing, 20, 21
    aligning activities with learning preferences tool, 22
    auditory-musical, 20–21
    bodily-kinesthetic, 21
    interpersonal, 21
    intrapersonal, 21
    logical-mathematical, 20
    verbal-linguistic, 20
    visual-spatial, 21
legibility, 83, 103
Lewin, Kurt, 71–72
lighting, 29–30
listening, 96, 118–119
logical-mathematical learning style, 20

## M

matrices (weighted decision tables), 73–74
media
    flipcharts, 80–83
    handouts, 87
    interactivity levels tool, 79
    presentation software, 83–85
    selecting appropriate, 79–80
    shared whiteboards, 137
    streaming media and live Internet, 85–87
    and technology planning checklist, 88
meeting(s). *See also* virtual meetings
    agenda, preparing an, 23
    audience profile, 18–22
    beginning the, 39–49
    characteristics of effective meetings tool, 17–18
    ending the, 145–148
    logistics, 25–31, 34–35
    objectives, accomplishing, 109–110
    selecting appropriate media, 79
    types, 12–13

metaphors and analogies, 101–102
mind mapping, 56–57
mule, 128
multivoting (nominal group technique),
    61–62
"mute" button considerations, 133

## N

noise outside the meeting, 30
nominal group technique (multivoting),
    61–62
nonverbal communication
    body language, 106–107, 108
    distractions, 107
    facial expressions, 108
    gestures, 107–108
    proximity to participants, 108
    reading the room, 103–104
    stance, 107
norming (stage 3 of team development),
    114

## O

objectives, accomplishing meeting,
    109–110
off-agenda items, 48, 93
offensive material, avoiding, 100–101
open-ended questions, 97
openers, 40–41, 132
orientation prior to a virtual meeting, 134,
    142–143

## P

parking lot for off-agenda items, 48, 94,
    109
participants
    difficult, 125–128
    expectations of, 17
    quiet, 11, 127
    and their responsibilities, 46
    virtual, photos of, 19
participation
    levels of, 53
    tips for encouraging, 94
patterns, finding, 58
people bingo tool, 43
performing (stage 4 of team development),
    115

personality problems, 127
planning for facilitation
    checklists, 34–37, 88
    creating an audience profile, 18–22
    meeting logistics, 25–31
    practicing before the meeting, 32–33
    preparing an agenda, 23
    pre-work, 31–32
    understanding the goals of the meeting,
        15–18
PowerPoint, 83. *See also* presentation
    software
practicing before the meeting, 32–33
presentation software
    design guidelines, 84
    projection options, 83–84
    specific software recommendations, 83
    when to use and when not to use, 84–85
presenters *vs.* facilitators, 7–8
pre-work, 31–32
problem solving
    classic group techniques, 9, 67–70
    criteria for an acceptable solution, 69

## Q

questioning techniques
    closed-ended questions, 98
    guided discussion questions, 99
    hypothetical questions, 98
    open-ended questions, 97
    rhetorical questions, 99
questions for learning client expectations
    tool, 16
quiet participants
    drawing out, 11
    the quiet one as a disruptive behavior,
        127
quotations, 101

## R

rambler, 126
readability of information, 83, 103
reading the room, 103–104
ready answer, 126
recording virtual meetings, 135–136, 138
reframing, 95
rehearsing before the meeting, 32–33
reverse brainstorming, 62
rhetorical questions, 99